Adult Drug and Alcohol Problems, Children's Needs

of related interest

A Practical Guide to Early Intervention and Family Support
Assessing Needs and Building Resilience in Families Affected by
Parental Mental Health Problems or Substance Misuse
Emma Sawyer and Sheryl Burton
ISBN 978 1 90939 121 5
eISBN 978 1 90939 130 7

Helping Children Affected by Parental Substance Abuse
Activities and Photocopiable Worksheets
Tonia Caselman
ISBN 978 1 84905 760 8
eISBN 978 1 78450 087 0

Child Protection, Domestic Violence and Parental Substance Misuse
Family Experiences and Effective Practice
Hedy Cleaver, Don Nicholson, Sukey Tarr and Deborah Cleaver
Foreword by Kevin Brennan
ISBN 978 1 84310 582 4
eISBN 978 1 84642 673 5

Risk in Child Protection
Assessment Challenges and Frameworks for Practice
Martin C. Calder with Julie Archer
ISBN 978 1 84905 479 9
eISBN 978 0 85700 858 9

Social Work with Troubled Families
A Critical Introduction
Edited by Keith Davies
ISBN 978 1 84905 549 9
eISBN 978 0 85700 974 6

Direct Work with Family Groups
Simple, Fun Ideas to Aid Engagement and Assessment and Enable Positive Change
Audrey Tait and Helen Wosu
ISBN 978 1 84905 554 3
eISBN 978 0 85700 986 9

Direct Work with Vulnerable Children
Playful Activities and Strategies for Communication
Audrey Tait and Helen Wosu
ISBN 978 1 84905 319 8
eISBN 978 0 85700 661 5

Parental Substance Misuse and Child Welfare
Brynna Kroll and Andy Taylor
Foreword by Jane Aldgate
ISBN 978 1 85302 791 8
eISBN 978 1 84642 290 4

Adult Drug and Alcohol Problems, Children's Needs

An Interdisciplinary Training Resource for Professionals – with Practice and Assessment Tools, Exercises and Pro Formas

Second Edition

Joy Barlow MBE, Di Hart and Jane Powell

Jessica Kingsley *Publishers*
London and Philadelphia

'Black and minority ethnic drug use' on pp.159–61 is reproduced with
the permission of the author, Dima Abdulrahim.

Every effort has been made to trace copyright holders and to obtain their permission for the use of copyright
material. The author and the publisher apologize for any omissions and would be grateful if notified of
any acknowledgements that should be incorporated in future reprints or editions of this book.

First edition published in 2007 by National Children's Bureau
This second edition first published in 2016 by National Children's Bureau
an imprint of Jessica Kingsley Publishers
73 Collier Street
London N1 9BE, UK
and
400 Market Street, Suite 400
Philadelphia, PA 19106, USA

www.jkp.com

Library of Congress Cataloging in Publication Data
A CIP catalog record for this book is available from the Library of Congress

British Library Cataloguing in Publication Data
A CIP catalogue record for this book is available from the British Library

ISBN 978 1 90939 125 3
eISBN 978 1 90939 129 1

Printed and bound in Great Britain

Contents

Acknowledgements

First edition

Thanks to the Department of Health for funding the development and publication of the original toolkit, now updated, and the following people, who generously contributed their time and expertise:

- Dima Abdulrahim, Specialist Adviser, National Treatment Agency

- Celia Atherton, Director, Research in Practice

- Dr Kath Burton, Associate Specialist in Community Paediatrics, and Medical Adviser to the Stoke-on-Trent Adoption Panel

- Brenda Celestine, Specialist Midwife, Camden and Islington PCT

- Valerie Corbett, Assistant Regional Director, Aberlour Trust

- Annie Darby, Specialist Health Visitor – Substance Misuse, North East Lincolnshire PCT/DAT

- Dr Mary Hepburn, Consultant Obstetrician, Princess Royal Maternity Hospital, Glasgow (retired)

- Caroline Little, Solicitor and Co-chair of the Association of Lawyers for Children

- Faye Macrory, Consultant Midwife, Manchester Specialist Midwifery Service

- Michael Murphy, Senior Lecturer, Faculty of Health and Social Care, University of Salford

- John Simmonds, Director of Policy, Research & Development, BAAF

- Jo Manning, Programme Manager, STARS project, Nottingham

- Julie Murray, DAAT Coordinator, Borders Drug and Alcohol Action Team

- Gill Watson, Parental Substance Misuse and Child Care Social Worker, Islington Children's Services/Mental Health and Social Care Trust

- all staff in the two pilot local authorities who shared their experiences and expertise

- and, finally, the children who describe their experiences so eloquently throughout the text.

Second edition

- Rachael Evans, Policy and Research Officer, Adfam

- Sue Bancroft, Independent Consultant and Trainer

- Elaine Wilson, Partnership Drugs Initiative and Strategic Support Manager, Lloyds TSB Foundation for Scotland

- Kelly McFadden, Partnership Drugs Initiative Project Lead, Lloyds TSB Foundation for Scotland

- Fyona Taylor, Partnership Drugs Initiative Intern, Lloyds TSB Foundation for Scotland

- Dr Lorna Templeton, Independent Consultant

- Vickie Ambrose for her technical expertise.

'I wasn't like a normal kid, all full of fun…' (13-year-old)

'We was all taken into care. No-one really explained it to us. I was ten. I was the oldest. They just said "it's because your mum takes drugs", and they put us in foster care.' (16-year-old)

'I missed a lot of school because Mum got her giro on one day and Dad got his on another. I had to make sure that I was at home when they arrived so I could get the money off them for food and stuff before they spent it all on drugs and drink.' (13-year-old)

'I used to wake up every morning in bed and worry that I'd find my mum dead in bed.' (11-year-old)

From: FRANK (2005)

'I wish someone would tell my mum the impact it's having on her family.' (12-year-old)

'I wish we had somewhere safe where we can go to quickly until things are better at home.' (10-year-old)

'Even though I was having them problems at home I didn't like show it at school. I'd still come in and do my work and act like a normal kid…I didn't let it show at all and I didn't say anything.' (10-year-old)

From: Adamson and Templeton (2012)

Introduction

Purpose of the toolkit

This toolkit is designed to support practitioners in their work with families where parents are using alcohol and drugs problematically. The first edition of the toolkit focused quite rightly on the impact of illicit drug use on parents' capacity and thus on children's welfare and safety.

In more recent years the impact of parental alcohol problems has been highlighted in both policy and practice.[1] In 2012 the Office of the Children's Commissioner (OCC) for England produced a seminal report *Silent Voices* (Adamson and Templeton 2012) which mirrored in many ways the findings of the Advisory Council on the Misuse of Drugs (ACMD) report *Hidden Harm* (2003, 2007). Subsequently the OCC has published a follow-up report considering the needs of children affected by parental alcohol problems at local levels (Manning, Clifton and McDonald 2014).

Thus this toolkit is also relevant in regard to parent alcohol problems, as these can have a considerable negative effect on children, young people and the family environment.

Whilst messages about parental problem drug use are transferable to alcohol problems, the second edition of this toolkit emphasises in a number of places the importance of assessment of parental drinking patterns and their impact on children (Hill 2011a). Many families will be affected by the wider patterns of problem substance use.

Many agencies become involved with families affected by drug and alcohol problems, which can add to the complexity of the task. The toolkit is aimed at all of them. Although the main practitioners are likely to be children's social workers and substance misuse workers, primary care and school staff often have a role, as do criminal justice agencies, obstetric or paediatric teams from NHS hospital trusts, and a wide range of voluntary and community services. Many children cannot live with their parents if the drug and/or alcohol problems are acute, and there may be substitute carers who are also in need of support. Their needs are also addressed within the toolkit.

---

1   Many of the messages are transferable, and readers may also wish to use resources published by Alcohol Concern to support their practice with alcohol-using parents.

Philosophy of care

It is suggested in many documents and research papers that the approach to care of children and families affected by problem alcohol and drug use needs to be:

- child-centred, focused on safety and wellbeing

- non-discriminatory, ethical and evidence-based

- holistic, based on an ecological model of family functioning and human development

- strengths-based, building on inherent resilience

- inclusive of a whole-family approach

- pragmatic, with an emphasis on reducing harm and promoting recovery

- coordinated, provided by a multidisciplinary and multi-agency team

- value-based, seeking to address health and social inequalities.

This approach is reflected in the toolkit.
The toolkit contains:

- summaries of the key messages for practitioners

- tools and tips to support effective practice

- useful information about a range of relevant topics

- training and development activities

- practice examples from around the UK.

Background

What do we mean by problematic use of alcohol and other drugs?

A useful working definition would be when the use of drugs and/or alcohol:

- is having a harmful effect on a person's life, and those around them

- may become the person's central preoccupation, to the exclusion of significant personal relationships

- is highly likely to be of a dependent nature – with significant impairment of health and social functioning.

Recognition in policy

Drug use by parents or carers does not inevitably lead to poor outcomes for children, but each aspect of their lives may be affected. *Hidden Harm* (Advisory Council on the Misuse of Drugs 2003) highlighted both the scale and seriousness of the problem. This report remains the seminal document from which both national and international work

on children affected by problem alcohol and other drug use has flowed. It∟
as follows:

- There were an estimated 250,000 to 350,000 children of problem drug
  the UK, about one for every problem user.

- Parental problem drug use can and does cause serious harm to children fɪ ⅎ
  conception to adulthood.

- Reducing such harm needed to become a major objective of policy and practice.

- Effective treatment of the parents has major benefits for the child.

- By working together, services can take practical steps to protect the children
  involved and improve their health.

- The number of affected children is only likely to decrease when numbers of problem
  users decrease.

In 2007 the Advisory Council on the Misuse of Drugs published *Hidden Harm Three Years On: Realities, Challenges and Opportunities*. The broad conclusions of this report were:

- A shift in policy and practice was identified and there was evidence of positive
  progress.

- A greater acknowledgement of the harmful effects of parental problem drug use
  was leading to better development of services.

- Some better outcomes for children were evident.

However, there were evidential concerns relating to:

- the need to build relationships between adult treatment services and child care,
  with a greater understanding of the complexity of drug dependency and parenting

- the requirement for clear leadership and cross-sector coordination

- the need for joint protocol development

- the provision of a range of dedicated services

- the importance of workforce development and training of all professionals involved
  with parents with problems associated with drug dependence and their children.

Similar concerns about children affected by problem drug use were raised in Scotland, and in 2003 the Scottish Executive published *Getting Our Priorities Right: Good Practice Guidance for Working with Children and Families Affected by Substance Misuse*. In response to the ACMD report the Scottish Executive also identified a range of actions (Scottish Executive 2006). In 2013 the Scottish Government issued an updated version of *Getting Our Priorities Right* which reflected the overarching policy of 'Getting It Right for Every Child' (GIRFEC).

Government responsibility for children affected by parental alcohol problems is much less clearly defined than that for those with problems associated with illicit drug use. This may lead to a lack of cross-government working; and a less than coordinated approach to alcohol policies. Nevertheless, the needs of children affected by parental alcohol problems should be further embedded within the children's agenda (Barlow 2011; Harwin 2010).

Given the common co-existence of alcohol with other problems, such as domestic violence or mental health problems, opportunities have been missed for different areas of policy to work together to consider better integrated working (Adamson and Templeton 2012).

Recognition in research

Children growing up in households where alcohol use is problematic often do not achieve their full potential in life. They may have low self-esteem, lack confidence, feel unsafe and find it difficult to engage in relationships, illustrating a lack of trust often into adulthood (Bancroft *et al.* 2004; Delargy *et al.* 2011). Alcohol misuse is also linked with family disharmony and violence (Velleman and Templeton 2007).

Evidence of the numbers of children in public care associated with parental alcohol problems is difficult to quantify. These brief statistics may help to give voice to the potential problems:

- It is estimated that over 1.5 million people in England and Wales are alcohol dependent (Department of Health and Others 2010 in Turning Point 2011).

- It is estimated that 30 per cent of children live with an adult 'binge' drinker, 22 per cent with a hazardous drinker, and 2.5 per cent with a harmful drinker (UK under 16 years – Manning *et al.* 2009).[2]

- Between 1999 and 2009 nearly 40,000 children calling Child Line raised the issue of parental (or other significant persons) drinking (Wales *et al.* 2009).

We also know that the children of drug-misusing parents are more likely than their peers to be included on the Child Protection Register or to become looked after, and a number of serious case reviews have noted parental drug use as a feature in families where children have suffered severe injury or death as result of abusive or inadequate care (see Cleaver, Unell and Aldgate 2011; Falkov 1996; Homila, Itapuisto and Iliva 2011; Reder and Duncan 1999).

Perhaps most importantly, we are increasingly hearing the voices of the children and adults with direct experience of growing up with parents or carers who use alcohol and drugs problematically, and a number of quotes from children are included in the toolkit. They provide a worrying picture of compromised care and inadequate emotional support, including, very importantly, examples of physical, emotional and psychological neglect. These messages are particularly challenging for practitioners, who share responsibility for safeguarding and promoting the welfare of children whatever agency they work for. It is not good enough for substance misuse workers to say that the child is not their 'client' or for children's social workers to say they do not understand the effects of alcohol and drugs on adult behaviour.

---

2   A 'hazardous' drinker is defined by a score of 8 and a 'harmful' drinker is a score of 16 or over on the Alcohol Use Disorders Identification List (AUDIT). This is a widely used standardised tool developed by the World Health Organization.

Need for knowledge and skills

In preparing the first edition of this toolkit back in 2007, we encountered many dedicated practitioners from all agencies who recognised the problems in current practice and were looking for support and guidance. Social workers told us that they had received very little training on drugs, yet were expected to cope with caseloads dominated by parental drug use. Substance misuse workers were unclear how children's services worked and were not sure how to contribute to assessments. These difficulties are found across all local authorities. Whilst time has passed since the first edition there is not a lot of evidence that matters have changed. Significantly, the work of Galvani and colleagues (Galvani and Allnock 2014) attests to the improvements required in alcohol and drugs training in pre-qualifying education and training. In 2015 Manchester Metropolitan University published *Alcohol and Other Drug Use: The Roles and Capabilities of Social Workers*. This generic document sets out key competencies in working with problem alcohol and other drug users:

- to engage with problem alcohol and drug users

- to motivate change in behaviour

- to support people in efforts to make changes.

STRADA (Scottish Training on Drugs and Alcohol), funded by the Scottish Government from 2001 to 2015, highlighted some improvements in the competency of specialist and generic workers particularly in the area of 'Hidden Harm'.

In order for the impact of alcohol problems on parenting, and thus on children, to be recognised, we need to improve our understanding and awareness of alcohol-related harm. Law (in Barlow 2010) concludes that alcohol is no ordinary commodity, and by raising our own awareness and challenging our own beliefs about alcohol we can thus open ourselves to the earlier identification of harm. Researchers have consistently noted the fact that social workers feel ill-equipped by their social work training to deal with substance use in their practice (Galvani and Allnock 2014; Galvani *et al.* 2011).

What is getting in the way of more effective practice? Some of the difficulties stem from the hidden nature of the problem, with both parents and children tending to conceal or minimise its impact to practitioners. It is important to take a proactive approach towards engaging families in order to undertake full assessments of the children's needs. The barriers to this may be:

- agencies' need to 'gate keep' rather than be proactive

- a tendency to be distracted by parents' problems

- the complexity of multi-agency working

- a lack of knowledge and skills in working with alcohol and drug issues.

There are also difficulties in care planning. The children of drug- and alcohol-misusing parents are over-represented amongst looked after children: although some are removed following assessment, many become looked after as a result of family breakdown or crisis after some years of poor parenting.

Decisions about whether or not a child can be returned home may be complicated by parents' imprisonment or substance use treatment. Substitute carers have anxieties about the children's health and development, about contact and about the child's risk of using substances. Extended family are often used as alternative carers, but studies have shown that this is not always the straightforward solution it might appear, and that there is an ongoing need for intervention (Barnard 2003, 2005). This is explored in more detail on pages 171–175.

The concept of 'recovery'

Since 2008 the UK government's Drugs Strategy (2015), and those of devolved jurisdictions, notably Scotland, have been based upon the concept of recovery from problematic substance use. UK and USA consensus groups (Betty Ford Institute 2007; UK Drugs Policy Commission 2008) and various government strategies define recovery from drug and alcohol problems as a process which is different for each person, and which has key components of overcoming dependence, maximising health, wellbeing, social integration, and contributing to society.

Little is known thus far about the impact of recovery from the child or young person's point of view. However, we can draw from work in the USA (Betty Ford Institute) and the Moving Parents and Children Together (M-PACT) programme that children can be assisted in a number of ways. These include:

- understanding the situation in which they have been brought up

- provision of a safe and supportive atmosphere in which to explore areas of change for them and their parents

- ability to express feelings about changed situations

- understanding of Mum and Dad being different from the way they were previously

- 'new' identities for themselves and their parents.

Projects such as M-PACT and derivations of Strengthening Families are being developed and delivered which explore practical ways to build family strengths, and to improve communication, relationships and the family environment. (See later sections 'Innovative practice' and 'Resources'.)

The Children of Drug-Misusing Parents Project

The Department of Health provided funding for NCB to undertake the above project between 2003 and 2006 with a view to highlighting the obstacles to effective practice and developing a whole systems approach towards the problem, and it still serves as a useful example for us to consider today. The project was concerned with those children who were 'in need' as a result of substance misuse and the response of agencies from the point of referral through to permanency planning for those who could not safely remain at home. These were the children in need of tier 3 and 4 services, and therefore where there was some involvement from children's social services.[3]

3   The term 'children's social services' will be used throughout to describe the service within local authorities responsible for the social work service to children and families.

Two local authorities were selected to work in partnership with NCB, and provided access to case files and staff in order for the project staff to gain an understanding of the key issues and to work together on developing their practice. One authority was a large county, and two locality offices within children's social services were selected for particular focus. The other was a small unitary authority. Interestingly, the issues that emerged were almost identical.

Project activities

MAPPING THE EXTENT OF THE DEMAND

Children's social services in both pilot authorities highlighted all new and existing cases where parents were identified as drug users between 1 January 2004 and 31 March 2004. These cases were examined to provide a snapshot of activity, including information about numbers of children referred during that time, children on the Child Protection Register and looked after children. The nature of the assessment, the outcome and any protection or care plans were also examined.

CASE STUDIES

The mapping was supported by ten in-depth case studies in each authority. Case files were examined in order to provide qualitative information about the work undertaken. Issues were noted, such as the information recorded about parental drug use, the involvement of other agencies in assessment, and the extent to which children were involved. In three cases, the information was supported by discussion with the social worker. A sample of family members were also interviewed, and their messages are presented later in the text.

INTERVIEWS

Interviews were undertaken with key personnel from across relevant agencies within each authority. These included social workers and managers, substance misuse services, obstetric services, designated health professionals, voluntary agencies and family centre staff. Views about the strengths and weaknesses of the service were sought, along with suggestions about what would help.

DOCUMENTARY ANALYSIS

The systems, policies and procedures that supported staff in their work were examined. This included the ways in which referrals to children's social services were processed, the forms used, and any protocols that were available to offer guidance to staff either within or across agencies.

DEVELOPMENT ACTIVITY

The findings from the above were fed back at a range of events and stakeholder meetings within each authority, and decisions taken about a programme of training or other activity that NCB would provide. These ranged from events for strategic managers from across the authority, input to the development of new policies and procedures, workshops with social work managers, training on assessment for social workers and multi-agency groups, and workshops for foster carers.

EVALUATION

The project was evaluated by NCB's research department. They collated the feedback from training events and followed this up by telephone interviews with a sample of participants some time after the events.

Key project findings

EXTENT OF PROBLEM

Both the pilot authorities were working with a high proportion of families where parents used drugs, in spite of their demographic differences. The families also shared many other difficulties, particularly domestic violence and mental ill-health. There were some differences in the pattern of drug use, in that the economically disadvantaged population in the small unitary authority were more likely to use intravenously, and to live in large families where several members misused drugs.

Overall, fewer than half of the relevant children known to children's social services during the study period were living with their parents, and there appeared to be little prospect of a return home for many of these separated children. Some children were formally looked after, but others were cared for by family and friends. The children accounted for an average of 18.5 per cent of the authorities' looked after population and 20 per cent of children on their Child Protection Registers. (NB: This does not include parents who are problem alcohol users.)

A STRATEGIC APPROACH?

Neither authority had an inter-agency strategy to address the needs of the children of drug-misusing parents, in spite of the extent of need or the recommendations of *Hidden Harm*. There were no formalised mechanisms for joint planning or service delivery, although individual staff had developed good working relationships. For example, the DAAT (Drug and Alcohol Action Team) in one pilot authority collects information on the parenting responsibilities of their service users (as recommended in *Hidden Harm*), but there is currently no mechanism for sharing this information or using it to plan services. Workers in both adult and children's services were aware of tensions arising from a difference in priorities, different timescales for involvement, and a lack of shared understanding about the tasks. Staff from a wide variety of agencies said that they would be keen to be involved in initiatives to make a difference to the service offered, and many helpful suggestions were made – some of which would not require additional resources.

POLICIES AND PROCEDURES

Practitioners did not feel that they were all working to a common policy either within or across agencies, and there was a consensus that specific guidance on the assessment of families in which there is problem drug use would be helpful. A particular problem within existing policies is the lack of a clear threshold for referral to children's social services and insufficient guidance about the roles and responsibilities of different professionals. Staff were left with queries about whether they should be undertaking a level of assessment themselves, whether concerns were serious enough to warrant referral to children's services, and what their subsequent role would be.

PRACTICE ISSUES

There were many examples of outstanding work, but the following barriers to child-centred practice were identified:

- **Incident-led approach.** The response to referrals sometimes focused on the specific incident that had brought the matter to attention, such as police involvement. Although many of the incidents were not serious in themselves, they could indicate a pattern of chaotic parental behaviour related to drug use that was not being picked up.

- **Initial rather than core assessments.** As a result of the above, there were sometimes a series of repeated initial assessments, whereas only a core assessment would really be able to uncover what life must be like for the children in the household.

- **Single rather than multi-agency approach.** Assessments tended to be undertaken solely by a social worker in spite of rhetoric about the importance of a multi-agency approach. Workers with knowledge of adult drug use could have offered valuable insights to support these assessments.

- **Lack of understanding about drug use.** Social workers did not always gather information about parental drug use and/or consider this information in terms of the impact on parenting. 'Drug use by parents' was sometimes written with no further explanation. Where information was elicited or volunteered by parents, it was sometimes accepted uncritically with little evidence that efforts had been made to check reliability. If drug workers had been involved they might have been more challenging and sceptical – or possibly have had a different view about the prospects for change.

- **Adult rather than child centred.** Assessments did not routinely consider the perspective of the child, who was sometimes 'lost' when workers were faced with the overwhelming needs of their adult carers. Most assessments referred to having seen the child, but there was little evidence of attempts to understand the experience of living with a drug-using parent.

- **Inconsistency of pre-birth planning.** This combination of incident-led and adult-focused assessment is particularly unhelpful for considering the needs of unborn children, and practice varied widely, sometimes within the same team.

- **Bureaucratic vs narrative records.** Forms and brief case recording can make it difficult to have any sense of the family's story over time, and there was some indication that social workers found it difficult to interpret the headings from the Assessment Framework to capture the essential experiences of drug-using families. There is therefore a risk of overlooking what is important.

- **High thresholds.** Children's social services' thresholds, or eligibility criteria, were consistently perceived as being too high. Other agencies expressed concern that the assessment service was too inaccessible at times or failed to give feedback when referrals were made. In turn, social workers felt that referrals were sometimes inappropriate or insufficiently detailed, for example saying nothing more than 'pregnant drug user'.

- **Reactive rather than proactive intervention.** Where children did become looked after or were placed on the Child Protection Register, this was usually the result of a family crisis or breakdown rather than assessment, and meant that some children became looked after at an age when their needs were more difficult to meet. Given that many parents will be reluctant to seek help from children's social services, and children may be reluctant to speak out because of loyalty, a proactive approach is particularly important.

- **Patchy support to carers.** Once children did become looked after, the prospect of rehabilitation seemed poor, and plans were made to provide them with permanency. A large number of the children were placed with family or friends, under a variety of arrangements. Support was particularly patchy to these carers, but overall, the particular needs of those caring for children affected by parental drug use had not been picked up.

Conclusion

The purpose of the project was to highlight areas for change. The lessons suggested that, in order to improve children's outcomes, the following are required:

- a multi-agency response, including

  - forums for agencies to talk to each other

  - shared policy and protocols

  - understanding of each other's roles

  - joined-up assessments/care plans

- confident and competent practitioners

  - substance use workers who understand children's needs

  - child care workers who understand substance use

  - carers with adequate training and ongoing support

  - all must share an ability to understand the realities of life from the child's point of view

- services that are family focused, including direct work with children

  - (see: A model for meeting the needs of children affected by parental drug use on page 29).

The conclusions of the project previously described are still relevant but it should be noted that there have been some innovations in policy and practice. These include:

- dedicated workforce development and some recognition of specialist knowledge and skill acquisition (STRADA and Adfam and the Substance Misuse Skills Consortium)

- opportunities for better integrated working, identifying the problems of 'siloed' thinking and working (*Getting Our Priorities Right*, Scottish Government 2013)

- more research on the impact of problem parental substance use, particularly with regard to alcohol problems (Adamson and Templeton 2012)

- reports of serious case reviews which have highlighted the risks of opiate substitution therapy and practical support for parents and professionals (Adfam 2014)

- more holistic child care policy which recognises the importance of the needs of children affected by parental alcohol and other drug problems (GIRFEC)

- programmes particularly targeted at support for children (FEDUP)

- resources for use with children, for example 'Rory' and 'Oh Lila!' (Alcohol Focus Scotland).

Nevertheless, with new policy impetus and changing organisational structures there is always room for continual improvement.

The remainder of the toolkit is designed to help practitioners reflect on their practice, increase knowledge and skills, and work together more effectively.

A model for meeting the needs of children affected by parental drug use

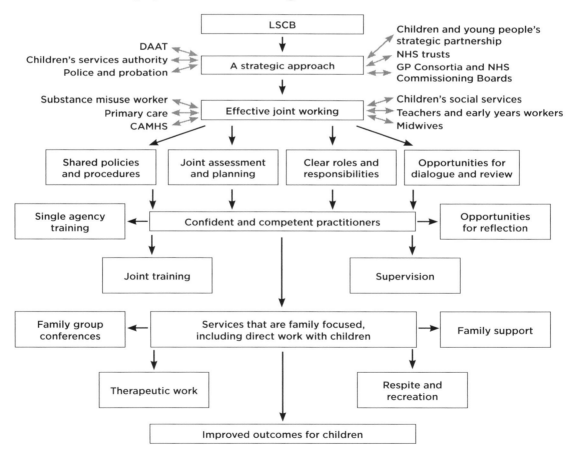

1

Key Messages

Recent research and policy

> While there remains a great deal to be learned about the consequences for children of parental substance misuse, the emerging picture suggests a very significant and sizeable problem, which is getting bigger, and which has a serious impact on child protection and looked after children systems. (Phillips 2004)

The publication of *Hidden Harm* (Advisory Council on the Misuse of Drugs 2003) focused attention on the experiences of the child of problem drug users. It contained a review of the literature to date, but information is continuing to emerge that should continually inform policy and practice.[1] Since 2003 a significant body of research literature has been produced which attests to the importance of the child at the centre of practice (Horgan 2011). As previously noted, the *Silent Voices* report adds significantly to the understanding of children affected by problem alcohol use of parents and carers. Some of the messages from research are summarised here.

Consequences for children

> For many children living with parental substance misuse, life can be difficult, dangerous and frightening. (Kroll and Taylor 2003)

Substance misuse may be just one of a series of inter-related factors within a family, such as poverty or depression, so that disentangling exactly what causes poor outcomes for the child can be difficult (Forrester and Harwin 2004). The SCIE *Research Briefing 06: Parenting Capacity and Substance Misuse* points out that studies have often failed to evaluate the impact of substance misuse on parenting capacity relative to other aspects of disadvantage (Social Care Institute for Excellence 2004). However, the research indicates that, whatever the primary cause of a parent's difficulties in caring adequately for their child, substance

---

1   Similar work has been undertaken in respect of parental alcohol use but is not covered here (Turning Point 2006, 2011).

misuse is likely to add to those difficulties. Work conducted by Dawe *et al.* (2008) shows the nature of taking an ecological approach to the consideration of consequences. This involves the child, family and community amply illustrated in the One World Triangle (Department of Health and Others 2000).

A number of studies have reinforced earlier findings both about the potential for harm and the resilience that some children display when exposed to parental substance misuse, but add a valuable dimension through being based on the testimony of those with direct experience: the children and families themselves. Overall, the message is that children are much more aware of, and much more worried about, their parents' drug use than is recognised by adults (see Gorin 2005). *Silent Voices* illustrates the lack of recent research on the unique features of living with parental alcohol misuse, though Louise Hill's work in Scotland is instructive. (*Silent Voices* also gives examples of areas of resilience to be explored.) What is known is that children living with parental alcohol misuse come to the attention of services later than children living with parental drug misuse. Boys are less likely than girls to seek help and are more likely to come to the attention of services with regard to their presenting behaviour, for example through Youth Offending Services, than for the harm they are experiencing.

For further information on the impact of problem alcohol use see *Evidence Base: Parental Alcohol Misuse* (Barlow 2011) and Community Care Inform (www.ccinform.co.uk).

EMOTIONAL IMPACT

Kroll and Taylor (2003) identified a risk to children's ability to form secure attachments if their carers were impaired by substance misuse, and that this could have long-term effects on their emotional health. This is confirmed by children, who frequently describe their lives as like 'walking on eggshells' or having parents who are 'not there for them' (Gorin 2005). Emotional absence and role reversals, with children having to become the carers for themselves, siblings and parents, is also a recurring theme in this and other research.

Interviews conducted for FRANK (2005) characterised the emotional effects as intense loneliness, constant worry about parents, anger and frustration, and guilt. A study of young people aged 15–27 who had grown up with parental substance misuse highlighted parental absence as a common experience, and young people could be burdened by anxiety as a result:

> 'And she'd just disappear and I was always scared in case she was…lying somewhere, dead or something.' (Bancroft *et al.* 2004)

On the other hand, the study also suggested that the impact on children of not being 'cared for' could be offset by a recognition that their parents still 'cared about' them. More recent studies, for example Houmoller *et al.* (2011), have also illustrated understanding that children have that they are loved but not cared for.

A recognition that children understand far more about their parents' problems than is acknowledged permeates the literature. 'They know but have never been told' (Barnard 2007). This may have profound consequences on emotional health in the future (Hill 2011).

PHYSICAL HARM

Many studies have found that violence and other forms of abuse were 'a common theme' in the responses of the young people interviewed and noted the extreme anxiety and fear of living with a parent whose behaviour could be unpredictable and dangerous. There were also physical risks from parents' chaotic behaviour: dropping cigarettes and falling asleep with electrical appliances on. Moreover, the dangers attached to substance misuse can come not only from the parent users themselves but the context in which they function:

> Children with parents or caregivers who are abusing drugs are also at a high risk for exposure to the 'drug using world' and its violent consequences. (Altshuler 2005)

Audits of Child Protection Registers have found that a significant proportion of children are living with parental drug and alcohol misuse (Cleaver 2007; Cleaver *et al.* 2011).

NEGLECT

Whilst an earlier study by Harwin and Forrester (2002) found a clear relationship between the pattern of concern regarding the child and the type of substance being misused, some concerns are the same whatever the substance involved:

> Neglect, however, was a unifying theme as whatever the substance used children seemed to be at risk. Emotional neglect can disable children from childhood through to adulthood. (Corbett 2005)

Young people describe parents' failure to shop or cook for them or living in a home that was 'like a squat really' (Bancroft *et al.* 2004). Where the young people tried to take on responsibility for household tasks, they could be undermined by parents' behaviour, such as 'dropping cans'. Neglect can be life-threatening (Brandon 2008), which means that chronic neglect cases should not be allowed to 'drift'. Recent work by Laslett *et al.* (2012) illustrates alcohol's involvement in recurrent child abuse and neglect cases.

MULTIPLE ADVERSITIES

There is a strong graded relationship between the number of childhood adversities experienced and a wide range of negative outcomes in adulthood. There can be significant effects of a single risk factor, but the accumulated number of risks have been found to be the most damaging and also predictive of higher probabilities of negative outcomes (Davidson, Bunting and Webb 2012).

Multiple adversities are noted as:

- poverty, debt and financial pressures
- child abuse/child protection concerns
- family violence/domestic violence
- parental illness/disability
- parental substance misuse
- parental mental health

- family separation/bereavement/imprisonment

- parental offending, anti-social behaviour.

(Lea 2011)

Children growing up in environments characterised by problem alcohol and drug use are potentially at risk of such multiple adversities.

SECRECY AND STIGMA

'They would call out "There goes the druggie's daughter" or "Your mum's a skaghead." Everyone else seemed to know, but we didn't.' (FRANK 2005)

'When she was taking drugs I used to block it out. I used to get slagged at school 'cause I didne have any good clothes and I was (called) a black neck (laughs) 'cause your neck wasn't washed... They used to say like my Ma was a junkie and all that to me as well.' (Barnard and Barlow 2003)

Social isolation, school disruption and fear of people finding out, or intervening and making a bad situation worse, are other recurring messages within young people's responses. One of the young people supported by the Aberlour Trust summed up the pressures: 'I just knew to keep it quiet...' (Corbett 2005). Silence and disclosure are now recognised themes in many children's narratives and compound children's emotional distress (Barnard and Barlow 2003). Yet if all the professionals involved with the family collude with the secrecy, even if well-intentioned, the child risks being unable to trust their own perceptions and may be confused and saddened as a result (Kroll 2004).

A related risk is that of the normalisation of drug use and offending behaviour so that young people may become users, and socially excluded, in turn (Kearney *et al.* 2005). Adolescence is a time of particular vulnerability in this regard.

THE IMPORTANCE OF FAMILY

Children, unsurprisingly, report very mixed emotions about their parents – anger, pity, contempt – but most do not reject them. There has also been recent research on living with siblings who use which suggests that this too can be harmful: children may miss their previous close relationship with siblings or feel pushed aside by the amount of family attention that the sibling use absorbs. Siblings may also introduce their younger brothers and sisters to drug use (Barnard 2005; Kearney *et al.* 2005). Family relationships can become distorted and problematic, but can also be an important source of support. Grandparents are particularly key in keeping children safe, either by stepping in at times of crisis or as permanent substitute carers. This may seem the ideal solution, but is not without its complications (Barnard 2003). Apart from the practical and financial problems that families may face, there are potential tensions arising from issues such as conflicts of loyalty. Parents may feel resentful of being usurped by their own parents, and perceive themselves to be under surveillance or judged. Grandparents still have emotional ties to their own children, no matter how problematic their behaviour, and may feel that they are making their drug problem worse by taking over the children's care and allowing parents to abdicate responsibility. These tensions will not be lost on the children:

'My nan was always on at us, always asking, like, "How is your mum? Is she looking after you properly?"' (FRANK 2005)

IN SUMMARY

- Children have a right to be listened to.

- Parental drug and alcohol problems can have a serious impact on all aspects of children and young people's lives.

- Children can have considerable knowledge about parental alcohol and drug problems from an early age; talking about parental problems and family functioning can be incredibly difficult due to family loyalty and the fear of separation.

- The majority of children show love and concern about their parents even in the most harrowing of circumstances; they may also feel angry, anxious and upset about their parents' behaviour, their use of substances and the impact in their lives.

- For some children basic needs may not be met, and there is a heightened risk of abuse and maltreatment. When children face multiple adversities over time, for example poverty, domestic abuse and parental mental health issues, then they are at greater risk.

- Children need someone to talk to, who they can trust and who is reliable.

What can be done to help?

EARLY IDENTIFICATION AND INTERVENTION

Research by Forrester and others emphasised the need for early identification and intervention (Forrester and Harwin 2011). This is confirmed in the Scottish response to *Hidden Harm* (Scottish Executive 2006), which said that planning how best to protect the child should start as soon as the mother's pregnancy is confirmed. The needs of vulnerable children already born should similarly be identified as early as possible, a responsibility shared by staff from all agencies. The Scottish Executive guidance also urged that interventions should be timely. Where meeting the needs of the child requires their removal into care it is important that 'the relevant decisions are made appropriately and permanent placements found quickly'. Following considerable research into early intervention which consolidated that of Forrester, the Allen Report (2011) provided further policy formulation across the jurisdictions of the UK. In Scotland, *The Early Years Framework* (Scottish Government 2009) and *The Early Years Collaborative* (Scottish Government 2015) identify the importance of all relevant professionals, including maternity, early years (health visitors), nursery and pre-school staff, working together to provide early preventative support for vulnerable children and their families.

Assessment is obviously useful in early identification if it identifies:

…which children need help and the level of concern, which aspects of development are being adversely affected and how, what services are needed to help both the child and family. (Cleaver *et al.* 1999, 2011)

THE SOCIAL WORK RESPONSE

In a study of the social work response to referrals of children with substance-using parents, Forrester and Harwin (2004) found that substance misuse of all kinds was a key feature in social work with children and families, but that staff received inadequate training and guidance. Unfortunately this situation is very little different today, despite work by a number of academics and agencies. Harwin and colleagues pointed to the absence of teaching about substance misuse within the new social work degree. This in turn contributes to social workers feeling isolated and poorly prepared when they are confronted with an instance of suspected substance abuse:

> …social workers require far more training in recognition, assessment of harm and above all, in making links between children's difficulties and the nature and severity of parental substance misuse. (Forrester and Harwin 2004)

Such training would help to replace an identified tendency towards misplaced optimism with 'realistic judgements about prognosis'. The authors also expressed concern about social services' pattern of reacting to acute incidents but failing to engage effectively with chronic concerns.

In Barlow (2010), Forrester contends that there needs to be a twin focus on professional excellence and evidence-based practice. He states that effective work with children and families affected by parental drug misuse is synonymous with effective work in general. He calls for a greater use of motivational interviewing, which is an 'exemplar of what can be achieved when there is systematic reflection on practice and outcomes which brings together practitioners and researchers' (p.118).

JOINT WORKING BETWEEN ADULT AND CHILDREN'S SERVICES

As with parents who have mental health problems, there are dangers of the child's needs being overlooked by agencies whose primary focus is on adults (Statham 2004; Gorin 2005). Taylor and Kroll (2004) comment on the tensions created by different agency priorities, objectives and protocols and the ways in which children can 'fall through the gaps'. Calling for more collaborative ways of working, they state that the potential for 'crossover posts' needs to be developed between children's and adult substance misuse services.

Professionals are seen as working in 'silos', with good intentions but with a focus on their specific client group. This has often resulted in the needs of children being lost in the plethora of adult needs (Munro 2011).

Collaborative competencies have been suggested as:

- describing one's role and responsibilities to other professions

- recognising and respecting roles, responsibilities and competence of other professionals

- coping with uncertainty and ambiguity

- facilitating inter-professional case conferences and meetings

- handling conflict with other professionals

- working with other professionals to assess, plan and provide care.

(Sloper 2004)

The recovery focus has brought into sharp relief the need to consider the whole family together and separately (Scottish Government 2012). This requires collaborative, coordinated approaches by all agencies involved, in partnership with parents and other family members as appropriate.

The welfare and protection of children requires:

- better communication and collaboration between and within agencies

- shared responsibilities across agencies for the identification and response to, the needs of and risks for children

- earlier intervention

- clear multi-agency assessments

- ongoing information-sharing

- a clear understanding of roles and responsibilities of all involved.

(Nicholson in Barlow 2010)

ASSESSMENT: GETTING THE BALANCE RIGHT

Various models have been developed to help professionals to undertake assessments where there are concerns about parental substance use (Kroll and Taylor 2003; Murphy and Harbin 2003; NTA 2005). More recently, with the emphasis on the recovery focus, assessment tools have been developed to take account of children's views and stages of parental recovery (Angus Council, *The Wellbeing Wheel*).

It is vital that those undertaking assessment understand the importance of the recovery agenda, whilst incorporating 'respectful uncertainty and compassion with sustained and dogged professional challenge…rigorous, systematic thinking and analysis' (Brandon *et al.* 2009). C4EO (n.d.) repeat the theme of demonstrating empathy and acceptance balanced with healthy scepticism.

Kroll and Taylor (2003) state that the assessment should look at the quality and 'feel' of the home environment; the patterns and effects of the substance misuse; whether it is the central preoccupation of the parent and what this means for the child. Murphy and Harbin (2003) point out that the picture will not be static: the needs of children will change over time, as will parents' capacity to look after them. The Scottish Executive stresses the importance of including the child's perspective:

What does the child think? What do other family members think? How do you know? (Scottish Executive/Government 2003, 2013)

Forrester (2004) suggests four key principles for undertaking assessments:

- first to focus on the child

- second to recognise that the adult's management of their own life is a good indicator of their ability to look after the child

- third that the best predictor of future behaviour is past behaviour

- fourth that information from a variety of sources is better than information from one.

Forrester suggests a 'risk and resilience' approach to assessing the likely effects of parental misuse. This would involve using research evidence and moving beyond information gathering to analysis. The Family Justice Review sets out clearly the need for social workers to use much more rigorous research skills in assessment (see briefing on Family Justice Boards, pages 170–171).

Work by Brown and Ward has highlighted the changes needed in decision making brought about by the Family Justice Review. More rigorous attention to timescales and the evidence base for decision making is evident from this review and indicates the importance of the supervision of cases and reflection on practice (Brown and Ward 2013).

There is now a much greater emphasis on whole family assessment following on from the My World Triangle (Department of Health and Others 2000) and the ecological approach already noted providing whole family risk assessment, including the inclusion of family members and exploration of the child's point of view. It is also relevant to consider the role of quasi-transient adults in a child's life, particularly where there are a number of people who may be described as 'putative parents'.

It is suggested that high levels of anxiety about risk may drive the search for the 'ideal' risk assessment tool, especially if it is used as an alternative to comprehensive assessment of all unmet needs (Vincent, Daniel and Jackson 2010).

IN SUMMARY

Elements of a good risk assessment are that it is:

- child-centred

- focused on actions and outcomes

- integrated in approach

- built on strengths as well as identification of difficulties

- a continuing process not an event

- transparent and open to challenge

- informed by evidence.

(Adapted from *Working Together to Safeguard Children*, HM Government 2013)

GIVING CHILDREN A VOICE

Children report not knowing where to get help: their 'most persistent plea' is that they need age-appropriate information to help them understand what is going on in the family (Gorin 2004). Despite the self- and socially imposed pressure to 'keep it quiet' noted by Corbett (2005) and others, children can find it helpful to talk:

> We thought it would be hard getting the children to talk, but in fact they are desperate to talk. They want to be heard. Many feel that they are overlooked by the system, so they are pleased when someone wants to listen. (Cosh 2004)

This was confirmed by the study for FRANK (2005). Children as young as five or six wanted opportunities to talk about their problems as well as to have some recreational and respite activities. There were not enough services that provided this. A number of agencies have developed materials to assist in undertaking direct work with children in these circumstances (McAleavy, Pearson and Sloan 2004).

Since the publication of *Hidden Harm* and subsequent policy steers there has been a significant increase in projects attempting to give children a voice. This work has been informed by a number of salient research and practice publications. These include:

- Barnard and Barlow (2003, 2007)

- Bancroft *et al.* (2004, 2010)

- Kroll and Taylor (2004, 2008)

- Houmoller *et al.* (2011)

- Hill (2011b).

PROTECTIVE FACTORS AND SUPPORT

Research over the years has made clear the importance of protective factors for children. These include:

- supportive family and friends

- understanding and vigilant significant others

- ability to find respite from difficult family circumstances

- sensitive teachers

- opportunities to meet other children

- participation in social activities

- space to talk with trusted adults.

(Adamson and Templeton 2012; Scottish Government 2013)

For parents, important factors include:

- contact with drug/alcohol treatment services

- supportive family members without alcohol and drug problems

- support in accessing/engaging with other services, for example housing, benefits, mental health, domestic abuse

- appropriate mentoring to demonstrate care for new mothers

- mother and baby groups

- consistent routines, for example meals, bedtimes.

Current developments

The need to tackle the problem has grown in prominence since the mid-2000s. Work from the Social Care Institute for Excellence (SCIE) draws together references to a number of policy and practice documents governing the provision of services to support parents who misuse substances (www.scie.org.uk). In Scotland, the Scottish Executive (2006) identified a number of key areas requiring further action, including:

- more effective and early identification of children at risk, including during pregnancy

- more effective communication between agencies, including sharing of information

- retraining of social workers and other front line staff in child protection

- ensuring that drug users with children undergo multi-agency assessment to assess parenting capacity and agree care plans with timetables

- a more interventionist approach to be taken by social work and related services, to ensure parental drug misusers comply with care plans and contracts

- a new national fostering strategy to help support the fostering option

- examination of governance, capacity and training for those working in this field, to ensure that they have adequate support and advice, and that everyone is clear about their respective responsibilities.

Much of this was drawn together in the update of *Getting Our Priorities Right* (Scottish Government 2013).

In England, the Children's Society established the STARS project in 2002 to provide a forum for both children affected by parental drug use and practitioners. It held regular forum meetings and provided a website offering information, support and practical materials. The initial Westminster government response to *Hidden Harm* was not as hard-hitting as that in Scotland, and the group monitoring its progress reported in February 2007. It demonstrated that the original *Hidden Harm* report had had a significant impact on policy at a national, regional and local level. Whilst impact was not consistent over all four jurisdictions of the UK there was evidence of positive progress. The report indicated the number of emergent projects and programmes begun under the auspices of *Hidden Harm*. A number of innovative projects have been evaluated in recent years and add to the understanding of work on better outcomes for children and their families. These include:

- The Family Drug and Alcohol Court

- Moving Parents and Children Together (M-PACT)

- Steps to Cope

- Parents Under Pressure.

(For programme and contact details see the 'Innovative practice' section in Practice Examples, pages 187–189.)

Public Health England (2015) in *Local Initiatives in Safeguarding* identify two examples in safeguarding and substance misuse in Lewisham and Sheffield.

Four areas are identified by Templeton (2013) as having some achievements of note. These are:

- recognising the size of the problem and its burden

- understanding how substance misuse can affect the family

- including children and families in policy

- developing a holistic response to meeting the needs of children and families.

In Scotland since 2001 a very considerable number of projects providing support for children and families affected by problem alcohol and other drug use have been funded through a partnership between Lloyds TSB Foundation for Scotland and the Scottish Government. This unique grant-making initiative, known as the Partnership Drugs Initiative, has produced reports, leaflets and briefing papers, as well as evaluatory data. It pioneered work on outcomes for projects and is currently exploring the impact of parental recovery from problem alcohol and drug use on children. Its work can be viewed at www.ltsbfoundationforscotland.org.uk.

It is necessary to reflect that some of the progress on *Hidden Harm* has been affected by significant changes in policy with changes to *Every Child Matters* and the advent of Getting It Right for Every Child in Scotland (see the briefing on Policy contexts, pages 170–171). Also changes in health service organisation and the introduction of integration of health and social care will continue to impact upon *Hidden Harm* policy and practice.

What has happened is that the original report has brought about impact on a worldwide scale, notably in Australia, South Africa and European countries, including Ireland.

Perhaps some of the most profound developments have been the recognition of the importance of alcohol problems in the family and the consideration of alcohol and drug problems from a children's rights perspective:

> According to the UN Convention on the Rights of the Child, children have the right to survive, to be protected from harm and exploitation, to develop fully and to participate in decisions affecting their wellbeing. In addition, they deserve respect, information, support and prevention services, and an opportunity to help determine how to attain a healthy future. Unquestionably, many of these rights are routinely undermined by problems relating to alcohol and drug use. (FORUT 2015)

The voice of experience
Parents' experiences

As part of the NCB project, some parents were interviewed. All those interviewed had been involved in care proceedings and had children no longer living with them. These are some of the points they raised:

- **We do want what's best for our children, even though it's painful.** If things are explained we can understand why decisions are made. Just because we can't look after our child doesn't mean we don't love them. 'From J's point of view what happened was the best outcome. We had our chances to look after her – and they were fair chances. I understand why the social worker set time limits – she was growing up so fast. It was the best thing for J to give her up…it wasn't the best thing for me.'

- **Don't judge us too quickly.** We're parents who happen to use drugs, as well as do lots of other things that parents do. It's not all right but we try to protect the children so they don't know and they aren't affected. Ask us about the sorts of things we do to keep the children safe.

- **Treat us with respect.** The way things are done is as important as what is done. 'I had to go to a hospital case conference in my nightie. I'd only given birth two days ago. I felt frightened and intimidated'; 'I had a male security guard outside my room and I was trying to breast feed.'

- **Be honest and up-front.** Tell us what you're worried about and what changes you expect. A written agreement would help. Tell us what we need to do, in what timescale, what help we'll get to do it and what will happen if we don't do it. And keep to your word. 'I was told if you do this and this and you work with us, then you can keep the baby. I did everything they asked of me and I still lost him.'

- **Take the trouble to learn about drugs.** It might also make social workers less worried and less likely to jump to conclusions. 'Social workers know nothing about drugs. They need to go on a course to learn about them. They never really asked me what drugs I did so thought I was worse than I was. The drug team were really good though.'

- **We need support and help too.** 'The baby had a social worker and the foster carer had a social worker but I had nobody'; 'After the court case they never came to see me again, or even got in touch. I was just left to get on with it.'

- **Indirect contact can be very difficult.** It sounds a good idea but it's very hard to do without support. What do you write? Especially when the letters are censored and there's a long gap between writing a letter and getting a reply. If we stop writing it's because it's simply too difficult, not because we've lost interest.

A grandparent's perspective

The following is based on an account given by a grandparent who was willing to share her story to provide some insight into the, increasingly common, experience of caring for a grandchild affected by parental drug problems. The names have been changed.

> When you've never been involved with social services before, you don't know what to expect. You read things in the paper and you have ideas about what social workers do and what they look like, but four years ago we weren't the sort of family that needed help from them.
>
> My daughter, Sam, got involved in drugs and was barely looking after herself. Then she became pregnant. It was a pregnancy full of crises as my daughter and her partner lurched from one dramatic episode to another – arrests, domestic violence, car crashes. Towards the end of the pregnancy Sam came to live with me for a while. There were days when I went out and bought her heroin to stop her withdrawing and the unborn baby from being hurt. It was one of the worst things I've ever done in my life, I was very frightened, but you do surprising things when you're desperate.

Jenny's name was put on the Child Protection Register at a meeting before she was born. I told everybody about buying the heroin because I wanted to be completely honest. We had a really good social worker then, called Margaret, and I still think about her. We had a contract with social services and a written plan about what was going to happen. When the baby was born, she and Sam would come and live with me and I would supervise her care. Sam had to come off drugs completely, to go into treatment first and not to use anything on top. And it worked really well at first. Sam was besotted with Jenny and I think she would have done anything for her. It was a very happy time for the whole family and one when it seemed that things might just work out. It started to fall to pieces when Jenny's dad came out of prison. Sam was given one last chance. The social worker told her she had to be drug-free and she had to leave her partner and if this didn't happen then Jenny would be given a permanent home and would probably be adopted. It didn't work out and it broke my heart when it was decided that Jenny was to go and live with an adoptive family.

I was sad when Margaret left. She had charisma, she was fair-minded and human, and very honest at the same time. She told us when she didn't know something, or wasn't sure, and she never said everything was going to be all right. She gave Sam goals and told her what would happen if they weren't met, so we all knew what the 'rules' were and where we stood. She spoke her mind and was an easy person to talk to – not judgemental. I felt at ease with her and felt that I could have told her anything. She was confident and knew about drugs, which is really important in these situations. She made it clear that she was for Jenny before anybody else, and I felt that she really cared about what happened to her.

The next social worker came from the adoption team. I found it more difficult to talk to her and felt as if she wasn't interested in my views or my importance to my granddaughter. Looking back now, I was terribly naïve, and didn't understand the care plan or what it meant to have a closed adoption. I'd looked after my granddaughter for over a year and thought I'd continue to have a role in her life. I felt excluded in a way that was cruel after all the cooperation and good relationship in the past.

My messages for professionals?

Be honest and clear about your plans. It is painful, but families can cope if we're included and consulted and understand why decisions are taken. Be flexible about contact with extended family. I was very important to Jenny, and she'll never know this. I would never have disrupted her adoption but I could have had a small part in her life and made sure that she knew she was a deeply loved baby.

Most people do what's best for children and are able to stand aside from their own feelings, but you can help by behaving towards us in a way that's respectful and honest.

A letter from substitute carers

This letter was written by two foster carers with experience of caring for babies who were looked after because of parental drug use. They both described their struggle to get recognition of the children's difficulties, and their search for ways to help them.

Dear Professionals,

The first time we looked after a baby who had been exposed to drugs before birth, we struggled to manage. Here are some thoughts from myself and another carer about what happened. We hope that it might help other carers in the same situation.

We do wonder if the behaviours of some children in the care system may be put down to their troubled upbringing, rather than symptoms of substance misuse by parents. Information about this does not often come to light or does so when, for us as carers, it is often too late. We may describe these children as being 'difficult to care for', without perhaps realising that so much of it was predetermined before they were even born.

We did not have problems with having our little one's behaviour accepted as part of his 'addiction' but found our health visitor at the time slow to react and apply for services. We had to ask for them ourselves. We were not prepared to 'lump' all his behaviours together under one umbrella, but attempted to work separately on each one. This way he received a far more targeted overall approach. It also became obvious that social workers had very little training about substance misuse. Awareness of the children's difficulties depended on their general experience. Their work tends to focus on court proceedings and assessments, and they can easily, but understandably, overlook the day-to-day strains that we foster carers have to deal with.

Carers need support and understanding. Sometimes just being listened to with a sympathetic ear can make all the difference, especially when it's accompanied with a determination to explore help and assistance for all involved.

Yours sincerely,

Foster carers

2

Practice Tools

The following section contains practical resources to support front line staff, managers and policy makers in reviewing and developing their response to the children of drug/alcohol-misusing parents.

Practice tip 1
Engagement and assessment

These suggestions are aimed at any front line practitioner coming into contact with adults who use drugs and/or alcohol, or their children.

- **Don't ignore drug and alcohol use**. But don't over-react either. This is something to be assessed. Be aware of the different attitudes between alcohol and drug use and potential under-reporting.

- **Use pre-birth assessments.** These can provide a valuable opportunity to engage parents, who are often very highly motivated to make changes in their lives.

- **Be mindful of the circumstances of neglect.** Neglect may be manifested as physical, emotional and social. It may be insidious and incipient and should always be continually assessed and circumstances not allowed to drift.

- **Remember that drug and alcohol users want to be good parents.** But be aware that their expectations may be too high: that the child will compensate for past unhappiness or provide an incentive to remain drug-free. They may set themselves unrealistic goals. This may lead to attempts to become abstinent too rapidly, with considerable risk of relapse. Be vigilant to the impact of shame and guilt experienced by many parents, especially mothers.

- **Consider the importance of drug and alcohol use in the parent's life.** If a parent's primary relationship is with a drug of their choice, then it will adversely affect their relationship with others – including children. If household resources –

financial, practical and emotional – are diverted to drug and/or alcohol use, there will be deficits for the children.

- **Ask for details of the drugs used and their effects.** 'Drug use' is not a single phenomenon but includes a wide range of behaviours. Specific information about the nature of drugs used, including alcohol (which may not be the primary drug of choice), and the lifestyle implications of such use, is needed in order to assess the impact on parenting.

- **Do not assume that abstinence will always improve parenting skills.** There may be risks of relapse, or parents may struggle to adjust to a drug-free lifestyle or relationship. Withdrawal from any form of drug can significantly impair capacity to tolerate stress or anxiety. Stability in treatment might be a more realistic option.

- **Find out whether alcohol or other drug use is the 'only' parental problem.** If so, then prospects for success are higher. Where there are multiple parental problems (e.g. mental health difficulties, domestic violence), then prospects of being able to offer safe and long-term care to children are significantly reduced. Drug use makes all other problems worse.

- **Base your judgements on evidence, not optimism.** If drug/alcohol use is enduring and chaotic, and there is no evidence of improvement, then this will undermine other interventions or support offered.

- **Be aware of your own views and feelings about alcohol and other drug use.** Consider how these might affect your judgements.

- **Recognise that parents are likely to be anxious.** They will worry about losing their children. This 'fear factor' is likely to lead to a reluctance to seek help or a denial or minimisation of problems. Children may share this fear of being separated from their parents.

- **Approach things from a strengths-based perspective.** Consider what strengths there are in the family network, what goals the parents have for themselves and their children. How do they feel about their inner resources of hope and achievement?

- **See life from the child's point of view.** What is life like when they wake up? When they go to bed? When parents are intoxicated or withdrawing? What is it like living in their family environment day after day? What are their hopes and fears? Who can they turn to? Use the 'soft' skills of assessment, which include active listening, observation of the environment and non-verbal communication.

- **Don't forget fathers/partners.** Assessment can sometimes focus on mothers, but others may have an equal impact on the children. They may also affect treatment outcomes if one partner is more motivated than another to address their drug problem. Remember that other people in the household may have both positive and negative effects on a child's safety and wellbeing.

- **Don't forget extended family.** They are likely to be a source of useful information – and may also be a vital support to the children. Family group conferences may make a real contribution to decision making.

Practice tip 2
Checklist for children's social work managers

- **What does this worker know about drugs and alcohol?** And what are their personal views and attitudes that may affect their judgements?

- **Is the assessment of parental drug/alcohol use adequate?** Does it provide a picture of the drugs used, how they are obtained, and the problems they cause? Informed knowledge about drug use is important because of the impact on behaviour, mood and lifestyle.

- **Does the information about alcohol and other drug use come from a reliable source?** Has information offered by parents about their drug use been accepted uncritically, and will it be necessary to consult with adult substance misuse workers? They too have a responsibility to safeguard and protect children in need and at risk.

- **Is the information complete?** Have all the key people with information been invited to contribute to the assessment? What is the nature of inter-agency working? Do the professionals trust each other's judgement?

- **What is the reality of life for this child?** Does the case file give you a real sense of the day-to-day experiences of *this* child living with *these* parents? Now and in the future? Has the child been seen and spoken to?

- **Does the assessment include partners?** And does it include non-resident partners or the child's father?

- **Have the extended family been invited to contribute?**

- **Is there an assessment of the impact of alcohol and other drug use?** There is likely to be an impact on the adult, on parenting, on the child, and on the context in which the family lives. Judgements need to be based on these, rather than on a simple description of what substances are used.

- **Is a core assessment needed?** Would it be more useful than a series of repeated initial assessments that add little information to what is already known? Response to referrals can focus on the precipitating incident and not take account of the holistic needs of the child. Remember the importance of the assessment of acute and/or chronic neglect.

- **Is there a useful chronology?** Individual incidents or referrals may not have been serious in themselves, but do they indicate a pattern of chaotic parental behaviour related to alcohol/drug use?

- **Has there been a genuine attempt to engage the family?** Or has the response to referrals been more about processing the case? Parents who use drugs will be scared of social work intervention, and children may be trapped in secrecy. Home visits are likely to be much more effective than office appointments, which may not be reliably kept. 'Warning' letters are pointless and may make things worse.

Practice tip 3
Thinking about care planning

- **Concentrate on the child, not the drugs.** Because of the parents' problems, there is a risk of basing the plan on their ability to become alcohol/drug-free rather than their ability to meet the child's needs.

- **Be realistic about the prognosis for the future.** The birth of a new baby or the initiation of care proceedings may well be a catalyst for change. But alcohol and drug use can be a chronic and relapsing condition. It is important to review the evidence and to avoid the 'rule of optimism' in order to protect the child – and parents – from attempts to keep the family together if they are not going to succeed in the long term.

- **Be clear about the purpose of a residential family placement.** This should only be considered if (a) it will tell you something you don't already know; or (b) there is a genuine reason to believe it will be successful. The assessment will always take account of the highly complex needs of an individual being considered for a residential placement. Don't use it as a safe place to fail or provide additional 'hard' evidence in order to support the application for a care order.

- **Planning for young children needs to reflect their needs and timescales.** These may be incompatible with adult timescales for demonstrating stability of drug use or abstinence. This aspect is particularly important in the era of recovery when parental change and growth may not match the needs of young children.

- **Children should always be the subject of twin track planning.** Concurrent planning (i.e. where short-term carers will provide permanency if rehabilitation fails) may be particularly useful if such a resource is available locally.

- **Consider using a family group conference.** This will help to engage the family in the plan. Even if this does not change the outcome, it will have benefits in maintaining the family's commitment and continuing involvement.

- **Be supportive of kinship carers.** Whilst such placements are likely to meet the child's needs, the complexity must be recognised. Issues around contact can be particularly difficult. The placements should be on a sound legal footing and supported practically, financially and emotionally. Don't withdraw support until/unless the child and family genuinely no longer need it.

- **Carers need full and honest advice from medical staff.** This should be offered prior to decisions about whether or not to take on children who may have been exposed to drugs antenatally. They need to know that there are gaps in our knowledge about the implications for children's future health.

- **Whose needs will be met by continuing contact?** Contact can be fraught if parents continue to use drugs – particularly if their use is unstable. It is important to keep contact under constant review to make sure the child's needs are central.

- **The child will continue to face challenges as a result of their experiences.** They may have to give up the habit of secrecy and to learn how to rely on adults; they may have to reconcile complicated messages about the moral worth of problem alcohol and other drug users or abandon unhelpful coping strategies.

Practice tip 4
Considering a specialist assessment

It is important to note that there is a changing commissioning environment which may well affect specialist assessments for services in a given area. There are different responses by services and systems and a broader set of outcomes than reducing substance misuse alone. Therefore knowledge of local commissioning guidance and service availability is vital.

A residential assessment may be suggested, particularly where the children are subject to care proceedings. Alternatively, a specialist assessment may be commissioned in the community. Such services may also include an element of treatment/intervention, for example drug rehabilitation or training in parenting skills. It is important that such assessments and interventions are purposeful and well planned. The following are things to consider.

- **What would the purpose of the placement/service be?** There needs to be some point to it, whether this is to provide essential information for assessment or to enhance parenting skills.

- **Is there a good chance it will succeed?** Is there sufficient information to suggest cause for optimism about the likely success of such a placement? Residential placements should not simply be provided as a safe place to fail.

- **Can the child wait?** There is likely to be a time delay in finding a residential placement and in arranging funding.

- **What is to be assessed?** If the main purpose of the proposed placement/service is assessment, exactly what are you trying to find out? Is it evidence about parenting skills and/or drug/alcohol use? Does this include prognosis for the future? Who will be assessed? Is it one or both parents? Or the child? Or the relationships between them?

- **How will this be better than assessment in the community?** A residential assessment will provide specific evidence about ability to provide 24-hour care, whereas a community-based assessment will provide more information about the family's ability to cope at home. Which is most appropriate for this particular family?

- **What are the alternatives?** Could information equally well be provided by a package of drug/alcohol treatment/psychiatric assessment/frequent contact?

- **Is the service culturally appropriate?** Consider the family's ethnicity, religion, language, social class and gender.

- **Is the service child or adult focused?** Are there appropriate facilities for children within the proposed placement/service? Will they be safe?

- **Who is the placement for?** If the placement/service involves a therapeutic element, who is this for? Is it really a drug rehabilitation service which children can also attend, or a parenting programme that accepts drug-using parents?

- **Are all the key family members included?** There is no point proceeding with the mother/children only if there are other adults who will have an impact on the children's welfare.

- **Is the placement able to do the job?** Does the placement/service have the necessary skills and resources to achieve its aims? If not, can it access these from elsewhere?

- **Can the family cope?** The placement/service is likely to make considerable demands of the family. Are these achievable? Don't set them up to fail.

- **Can change be sustained?** And if so, what support will be needed?

Practice tip 5
Suggestions for foster carers

Some foster carers may have worries about looking after children whose parents are alcohol or other drug users. Carers have told us that they, and their link-workers, sometimes had little knowledge or experience. Looking after young babies straight from hospital after they had been treated for withdrawal symptoms was felt to be particularly difficult.

The following tips are from groups of foster carers who have been in this situation. They were asked what advice they would give to other foster carers. This is a list of their suggestions.

- **Get as much information as you can.** You will need to know about the baby's background and family circumstances, and the plans of children's social services.

- **If possible, visit the baby beforehand in hospital.** Find out about any medical problems, treatment and follow-up. Ask about their routine, likes and dislikes, and how they can best be comforted. You need information about the signs and symptoms of withdrawal and what to be worried about. Some hospitals use a score chart: ask them to explain it to you.

- **Once home, adapt to the needs of the baby.** They might not like bright lights or loud noises or being startled. Often the babies like being carried around in a sling. Even once they are free of medication the babies can be very unsettled, and difficult to feed and pacify.

- **Find out about alcohol and drugs.** An alcohol and drug awareness course will be useful, particularly if you're being asked to judge if parents or other adults are intoxicated when they visit. It is also important, as with colleagues with whom you may be collaborating, to look at attitudes and values.

- **Learn about handling the baby.** Babies can become very stiff and uncomfortable when they have been withdrawing. Gentle massage with baby oil will help this. Try and encourage them to open their hands.

- **Try to avoid judging the parents.** Parents will often be very sensitive to any perceived criticism, and feel judged simply on the basis of their substance use. Don't be drawn into any conversations where you are asked to express any personal views about problem alcohol and other drug use.

- **Don't take things personally.** Parents can often feel very guilty about their baby withdrawing, and these painful feelings can come out as being angry or critical.

- **A sense of humour will help.**

- **Be very clear about the contact arrangements.** Ask what the plans are in relation to who can have contact, and what to do if adults are late or you have concerns about safety.

- **Don't forget that you are an important source of information.** You have a vital part to play in planning for this baby. Even if they go home, your diary or contact notes or photographs may be the only record of this time in their life.

- **If you are not sure about anything, ask.** If you feel you are not being listened to, persist. Make a nuisance of yourself if you have to. Babies who have been withdrawing may continue to show subtle symptoms for a long time afterwards.

A model for assessment

One of the key challenges for social workers and partner agencies is to reach a judgement about the needs of children living with parents or carers who misuse drugs and/or alcohol. Although some children can and do thrive in such families, *Hidden Harm* and the voices of children themselves alert us to the increased risk of harm and poor outcomes. Even where parents are working hard to protect their children from the impact of their problem alcohol and other drug use, the associated problems faced by alcohol/drug users may mean that services are needed to support the child's development.

The framework for assessment would seem particularly useful for assessing such families because there are likely to be factors within all the domains – the child's developmental needs, parenting capacity and wider family or environment – that are affected by problem alcohol and other drug use. Similar domains are also included within the Common Assessment Framework which will be used by all agencies who may have concerns about a child.

Yet, in practice, there are a number of barriers to good assessment. These include:

- secrecy and denial, with both parents and children tending to conceal or minimise the drug use of choice

- children's social services' need to 'gate keep' rather than be proactive

- a tendency to be distracted by parents', often extensive, problems

- the complexity of multi-agency working

- lack of knowledge and skills in working with drug/alcohol issues.

This can result in assessments not being done at all or failing to get to grips with the children's true needs. The following model of assessment is an attempt to support practitioners from all agencies in applying the dimensions of the Assessment Framework (Department of Health and Others 2000) to families where children may be in need as a result of parental drug misuse.

Features of the assessment model

The model is designed to be a prompt to thinking, not a checklist. It:

- offers a way of interpreting the Assessment Framework rather than replacing it or adding additional tasks

- aims to offer a systematic approach towards assessment based on the particular issues that *may* be relevant in families where parents use drugs and/or alcohol problematically

- will reveal family strengths as well as difficulties: for example, many grandparents are a caring and reliable presence in the lives of children affected by parental problems, and may step in to meet the child's needs when times are hard

- will guide multi-agency groups in assigning assessment tasks because it highlights specific questions that different practitioners will be best placed to answer

- provides a transparent approach which will help to engage children and families

- encourages a holistic and child-centred rather than an incident-led approach.

Using the model

The following pages include a diagram indicating how the Assessment Framework triangle could be applied, followed by a table offering a fuller explanation.

- The model follows the dimensions round the triangle and raises issues that may impact on each one.

- The issues are not exhaustive but are designed to help to guide conversations with other agencies and the family.

- Wherever possible, and certainly in core assessments or s47 enquiries (where a child may be suffering, or is likely to suffer, significant harm), the assessment should be planned with the family themselves and with all practitioners who have information to contribute:

  ◦ This will highlight the information already available and the gaps that need to be filled.

  ◦ Tasks can then be assigned in order to fill those gaps. This will avoid unnecessary or duplicate enquiries being made.

  ◦ It will be particularly important to establish who is going to talk to the child and help them to understand the process.

  ◦ The way in which the information will be analysed and conclusions fed back should also be agreed.

- Children and parents should be fully involved, and family group conferences may be a useful means of achieving this.

NB: Remember that there will be many other aspects of the child's life that are nothing to do with drugs and may be equally or more important. These must also be assessed.

APPLYING THE ASSESSMENT FRAMEWORK

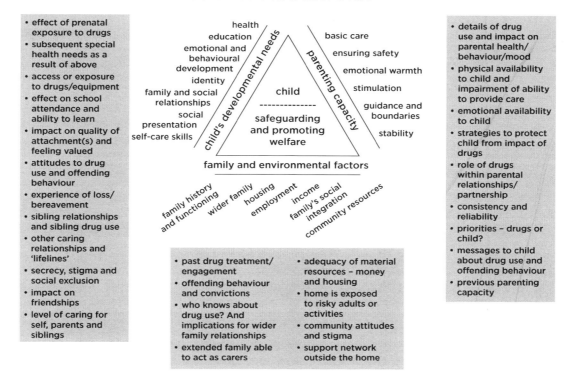

- effect of prenatal exposure to drugs
- subsequent special health needs as a result of above
- access or exposure to drugs/equipment
- effect on school attendance and ability to learn
- impact on quality of attachment(s) and feeling valued
- attitudes to drug use and offending behaviour
- experience of loss/ bereavement
- sibling relationships and sibling drug use
- other caring relationships and 'lifelines'
- secrecy, stigma and social exclusion
- impact on friendships
- level of caring for self, parents and siblings

- details of drug use and impact on parental health/ behaviour/mood
- physical availability to child and impairment of ability to provide care
- emotional availability to child
- strategies to protect child from impact of drugs
- role of drugs within parental relationships/ partnership
- consistency and reliability
- priorities – drugs or child?
- messages to child about drug use and offending behaviour
- previous parenting capacity

- past drug treatment/ engagement
- offending behaviour and convictions
- who knows about drug use? And implications for wider family relationships
- extended family able to act as carers

- adequacy of material resources – money and housing
- home is exposed to risky adults or activities
- community attitudes and stigma
- support network outside the home

EXPLANATION OF THE ASSESSMENT FRAMEWORK TABLE

- The dimensions from the Assessment Framework are listed, within the three domains.

- The factors that may have an impact are suggested. They do not necessarily relate to a single dimension, but are set out to correlate as far as possible.

- Suggestions are made about possible sources of information for each factor, either through direct assessment or collating information from others. Children and parents are the experts on their own situation, and should be invited to contribute fully. Where their views and experiences are particularly crucial, they are mentioned alongside practitioners as a reminder of this.

- It will be important to identify who within each agency is going to seek and provide the information. For example, a designated teacher or classroom assistant may know the child well and be better placed than the head teacher to talk to them.

- This is not a checklist but a way of signposting potential concerns.

ASSESSMENT FRAMEWORK TABLE

Child's developmental needs

Dimension	Factor	Rationale	Sources of information
Health	Effect of prenatal exposure to drugs and alcohol	Exposure to drugs and alcohol during the pregnancy may have an effect on the child's health before and after birth. It is important to consider whether the mother has attended for antenatal care and followed advice to reduce the potential risk to the baby. The baby may suffer from withdrawal syndrome at birth, requiring treatment in special care, which may in turn affect attachment relationships.	Substance misuse service Obstetrician Midwife Paediatrician Special care unit Primary care
	Subsequent special health needs as a result of above	The child may need follow-up to monitor for any special health needs. These may not be obvious immediately and will only become evident as the child develops. It will be important to consider both the child's needs and parents' ability to meet them. This is especially true of foetal alcohol spectrum disorder.	Paediatrician Midwifery and neonatal staff Substance misuse service Primary care
	Access or exposure to drugs/ equipment	Drugs and needles are a potential serious hazard to young children. A number of babies die every year from taking their parents' methadone. It is vital to establish what drugs are used, whether needles are used, and whether they are kept safely.	Substance misuse service Primary care Parents
Education	Effect on school attendance and ability to learn	Attendance at school and nursery may be adversely affected if parents are under pressure as a result of drug/alcohol use. Alternatively, children may attend but be hindered from learning because of problems at home. For other children, school is a vital factor in developing self-esteem and resilience. It may be difficult for them to talk about parents' drug use.	School/nursery School nurse Child
Emotional and behavioural development	Impact on quality of attachment(s) and feeling valued	For secure attachments to be developed with caregivers, they need to be consistently responsive to the child. Parents also need to be attentive to make the child feel loved and important. This process may be impaired if substance use has an effect on parents' availability or mood and behaviour.	Child School/nursery CAMHS
	Experience of loss/ bereavement	Children of alcohol/drug-using parents are at increased risk of loss, bereavement and separation. Parents may die or develop serious health problems; they may spend time in hospital or prison. Because the family is under stress, there is also greater risk of parental separation or family breakdown. It is important to explore such losses – or fear of loss in the future – and to understand the impact on the child.	Child Parents Family CAMHS

Dimension	Factor	Rationale	Sources of information
Identity	Attitudes to drug use and offending behaviour	The children of drug users may be receiving confusing and potentially harmful messages about the acceptability of drug use and offending. Loyalty towards parents may be at odds with drug education or media portrayals of drug users. This is a potential challenge to the child's identity.	Child Parents Teacher(s) Support services
Family and social relationships	Sibling relationships and sibling alcohol/drug use	Children living with parents who use drugs and/or alcohol to excess are at increased risk of becoming alcohol/drug users themselves. This means children may be living with siblings who are using and there are indications that they may become involved in turn. Alternatively, siblings may have close and protective relationships, or have become isolated from each other.	Parents Children Family CAMHS Youth services Substance misuse service
	Other caring relationships and 'lifelines'	Children will have a network of relationships, some of which may be compensating for parental problems. It will be important to explore and understand the roles filled by these relationships, and particularly whether anyone serves as a lifeline for the child at times of crisis. Such relationships can help to support the ongoing development of resilience.	Child Family CAMHS
	Impact on friendships	Children may be inhibited from developing supportive peer relationships by parental alcohol/drug use. They may be embarrassed by their parents' behaviour or other children may be told not to play with them. Friendship could also be a vital source of support, particularly if they are able to share their experiences or friends' homes provide a sanctuary.	Children Parents School/nursery Youth services
Social presentation	Secrecy, stigma and social exclusion	Serious drug and alcohol use is not socially acceptable, particularly for women, and users will worry about being judged 'bad' parents. They may also worry about other adverse consequences if their drug use is exposed. In turn, children may be worried about being taken into care or their parents getting into trouble if they talk about it. Drug users may be shunned within their community, and their children may share in this social exclusion.	Children Families School/nursery Support services Housing agencies
Self-care skills	Level of caring responsibility for self, parents and siblings	Children may become 'young carers' because of the parents' problems. They may have to take on excessive responsibility for themselves, siblings and parents. This may be apparent in terms of physical caring, but the extent to which children also feel emotionally responsible should also be considered. For example, some children feel responsible for helping parents tackle their alcohol/drug problem or for protecting them from stress so that they do not relapse.	Children Parents Family School Support services CAMHS

Parenting capacity (NB: It is important to consider all those with parental/caring responsibility towards the child. Research indicates a tendency to focus on mothers)

Dimension	Factor	Rationale	Sources of information
Basic care	Details of alcohol/ drug use and impact on parental health/ behaviour/ mood	It is important to understand the nature and pattern of parental alcohol and/or drug use in order to make judgements about the impact this will have on parenting. For example, crack use and alcohol may lead to volatile behaviour whereas heroin use is more likely to lead to drowsiness. Other relevant information will be how the drugs are obtained and funded, whether there are associated health problems, particular times of day when parents are likely to be affected by their use.	Parents Substance misuse service GP Police/probation
Ensuring safety	Physical availability to child and impairment of ability to provide care	Alcohol and other drug use may reduce parents' ability to provide physical care to the child. They may be absent from the home raising the money for or buying drugs, or in prison/hospital. Alternatively the effects of the drugs may mean they can't handle the child safely or react to protect them from danger.	Parents Substance misuse service Primary care School/nursery
Emotional warmth	Emotional availability to child	Similarly, the problems caused by alcohol/drug use may reduce the amount of attention parents can give to their child. They may also be distracted, drowsy or bad-tempered, depending on the drugs used, and unable to make the child feel loved or valued.	Parents Substance misuse service Primary care School/nursery
Emotional warmth	Priorities – drugs or child?	The use of substances, particularly if there is a physical dependency, can be an all-consuming activity that leaves little space for parenting. This may result in children feeling that their parents care more about the drugs than them. When assessing parenting capacity, it needs to be considered whether this is supported by an examination of their behaviour. Do they miss events at school or birthday celebrations because of drugs/alcohol?	Parents Children School/nursery
Stimulation	Strategies to protect child from impact of alcohol/ drugs	Parents may be well aware of the possible impairment to their parenting capacity and have developed ways of compensating for this. For example, they may draw on support of the extended family, or limit their alcohol and/or other drug use to times when the child is in bed.	Parents Family Support services
Stimulation	Consistency and reliability	One of the difficulties in assessing the impact of substance use is its fluctuating nature. Parents may be loving most of the time, but aggressive or irritable after stimulant use. They may make promises to the child when stable in treatment but break them when they relapse. It is important to understand these variations because of the disruptive impact on a child of having parents they cannot rely on to be there for them.	Substance misuse services Parents Family Child

Dimension	Factor	Rationale	Sources of information
Guidance and boundaries	Role of alcohol/ drugs within parental relationship/ partnership	It is likely, though not universal, that both parents will be involved to some extent in drug use. If so, drugs will play a central part in the relationship. One partner may rely on the other to raise the money or procure the drugs. This may be problematic if one partner is motivated to stop. Whatever the dynamic, it needs to be understood if assessing parents' ability to work together to look after the children. The relationships in heavy alcohol-using households may be very complex, with examples of co-dependency exacerbated potentially by violence.	Parents Substance misuse service Police/probation
	Messages to child about drug use and offending behaviour	Most drug use is illegal in itself and parents often need to engage in illegal activity in order to fund it. They may be involved with the criminal justice system as a result. Meanwhile children will be receiving messages outside the home about the fact that such behaviour is wrong. Parents will need to help their children make sense of this potential confusion. Children whose parents use alcohol excessively may be confused by the fact that alcohol is widely available and everyone seems to take a drink.	Parents Children School Youth services
Stability	Previous parenting capacity	A high proportion of drug users do not have their children living with them. Such children are also more likely to be on the Child Protection Register. It is important to obtain full information about the wellbeing of any previous child that either parent has cared for and to consider whether there are any lessons to be learned. The areas of potential supports for recovery should be examined. Have there been periods of abstinence; if so what helped to achieve this? Have they used self-help or mutual aid? Parents should be encouraged to consider their strengths as parents and their goals for their children.	Parents Family Other social services departments

Family and environmental factors

Dimension	Factor	Rationale	Sources of information
Family history and functioning	Past alcohol/ drug treatment/ engagement	If assessing the capacity for parents to change, it will be important to consider each parent's drug history and the effectiveness of previous treatment. Relapse is common, but the overall trend may indicate whether the drug/alcohol problems are getting better or worse. The motivating factors that prompted treatment, the level of engagement, the nature of the treatment and the outcome will all be relevant in assessing the likelihood of future treatment being effective.	Parents Substance misuse service Primary care Probation
	Offending behaviour and convictions	Many drug users will have become involved with criminal behaviour, either directly through the possession or selling of illegal substances or indirectly through crime to fund drug use. They may be facing new or unresolved charges. It is important to know about the types of crime committed and any outstanding charges, particularly if there is a likelihood of custody, in order to assess the likely impact on the children. Children may be harmed by certain types of offending behaviour or they may be facing the loss of parents to a prison sentence.	Police/probation Substance misuse service Parents
Wider family	Who knows about drug use? And implications for wider family relationships	Because of the level of secrecy and stigma attached to drug use, it is important to establish who knows about it. Parents may think that no-one knows, particularly their children, but this may not be the reality. If the drug use is not openly acknowledged, the children may be hampered from discussing their experiences and from seeking help. Family and friends may find it difficult to offer support if the problem is denied. On the other hand, if everyone knows, the family may be stereotyped unfairly.	Parents Children Family Support services
	Extended family able to act as carers	Many families are able to meet the needs of children because of support from the extended family. Children may live with family members some or all of the time, or family may intervene behind the scenes to make sure children get extra help practically and emotionally. This may be complicated, however, with parents feeling judged and undermined. Children may be confused, or have conflicts of loyalty as a result. Services may also have unrealistic expectations about the role of extended family and provide inadequate support. Assessments should recognise the potential of extended family, but realise the heavy demands and difficult family dynamics this may cause.	Family Parents Child Support services Family group conferences

Dimension	Factor	Rationale	Sources of information
Income, employment, housing	Adequacy of material resources – money and housing	Drug and alcohol use is a major drain on a family's resources. Money might be diverted from essentials such as food to buy drugs, or it may mean that there is nothing left to give the children outings and the same standard of living as their peers. This may be felt more acutely by older children and adolescents. Parents may also be too compromised by their drug problem to maintain the home or make it a good environment for the children to be in. Drug users tend to have less stable housing than others, and may lose tenancies because of their problems.	Housing agencies Substance misuse services Support services
	Home is exposed to risky adults or activities	Parents may have few contacts except other drug users. If compelled to engage in crime to fund their drug use, they may be selling drugs or become involved in the sex industry. This may result in visitors to the home who pose a risk to the children, or adults being unable to control what goes on in the home.	Housing agencies Police/probation Neighbours
Family's social integration	Community attitudes and stigma	If the family have been labelled as drug users within their community, they may be demonised and rejected. This rejection may extend to the children but they will also be hurt by their parents' social exclusion. On the other hand, some communities contain a high proportion of drug users, and the children may experience a subculture that exposes them to drug use as a way of life. It is important to understand how the family fit into their particular community.	Housing agencies Neighbourhood projects Sure Start
Community resources	Support network outside the home	Communities, schools and support services may be available to support the child and their family in a variety of ways. A school with good pastoral support may have breakfast or after-school clubs that provide stimulation and someone to take an interest. Youth services may be able to help children have some fun and develop their skills and self-esteem. There may be specific services such as young carers' groups or family support that help the family to build on their strengths. Or there may be a degree of empathy and acceptance from neighbours or the parents of school friends. All of these may help the family to cope.	Schools Youth services Voluntary sector Targeted services

Auditing social work practice
Purpose

Given the quantity of work being undertaken by children's social services and the continuing concern about the children's outcomes, it may be useful to undertake internal audits to look at the nature and quality of the work being undertaken. This could be done within authorities or teams, looking at a sample of cases, or within individual supervision.

Planning the audit

It will be important to establish the process for undertaking the audit and responding to the findings, linking with other arrangements for quality assurance and accountability. This is likely to include specialist staff, such as child protection advisers or independent reviewing officers. It should be acknowledged to staff that this is a difficult and complex area of work, for which many practitioners have received little training. It is important that the exercise is not used to criticise the practice of individual practitioners but to identify any areas for improvement. The exercise will therefore work best if it is undertaken in a climate of openness and self-reflection. It will be particularly important to establish what will happen as a result of the audit:

- Who will report on the findings?

- Who will the report go to?

- Will individual cases/practitioners be identified (or identifiable)?

- Will the social worker concerned have an opportunity to contribute their views or comment on the accuracy of the conclusions drawn?

- How will any need for action be taken forward?

It must be remembered that the audit will provide only one dimension: what has been recorded in case files. This may not fully reflect the work that has been done. It will be important to seek other information – by talking to the children, families and staff directly involved.

Process

The following audit form can be used to review all, or a sample, of case files concerning the children of drug-using parents. It is important to complete a separate form for each child to ensure that their individual needs have been considered, even where there are several children in the family.

Most of the questions require the auditor(s) to exercise their subjective judgement about the quality of the work undertaken, but prompts are included to help inform these judgements.

Several people working together should ideally undertake the audit, so that judgements can be shared and checked for consistency. The exercise can be a learning experience in itself, as it may highlight aspects of the work that can be overlooked when considering cases in isolation.

See also Practice tips, pages 44–51.

RESOURCE CASE AUDIT TOOL: CHILD AFFECTED BY PARENTAL ALCOHOL/DRUG MISUSE (page 1)

Household

Child's index no.	DOB or EDD	Ethnicity	Relationship to child	P.R. Y/N	Living with child?

Details of most recent referral

Date of referral

Who referred?   Name   Agency/role

Reason for referral

Brief description of background, including previous referrals

Response to referral

Action	Date(s)	Comments
No action		
Advice/referred on		
Initial assessment		
Core assessment		
Strategy meeting		
s47 enquiry		
Case conference		Registered ☐ Yes ☐ No Category:
Other meeting		
Legal proceedings		
Comment		

RESOURCE CASE AUDIT TOOL: CHILD AFFECTED BY PARENTAL ALCOHOL/DRUG MISUSE (page 2)

Which other professionals were involved in the assessment?

Health visitor	☐ Yes ☐ No	Nursery/early years	☐ Yes ☐ No
GP	☐ Yes ☐ No	EWO	☐ Yes ☐ No
Midwife	☐ Yes ☐ No	YOT	☐ Yes ☐ No
Substance misuse worker	☐ Yes ☐ No	Community mental health	☐ Yes ☐ No
Paediatrician	☐ Yes ☐ No	Hospital	☐ Yes ☐ No
Obstetrician	☐ Yes ☐ No	Foster carer	☐ Yes ☐ No
Psychologist	☐ Yes ☐ No	Other LA SSD	☐ Yes ☐ No
School	☐ Yes ☐ No	School nurse	☐ Yes ☐ No
Police/probation	☐ Yes ☐ No	Other – specify	☐ Yes ☐ No

What was the assessment process?

Contact with parents/carers. *Include fathers/partners as well as mothers. Who was spoken to? Home visit or office appointment? Were they given written information?*

Contact with family/friends. *Include paternal and maternal family. Who was spoken to? Home visit or office appointment? Were they given written information?*

Child(ren). *Was the child seen/spoken to? Were siblings seen/spoken to? Home visit or office appointment? Were they seen alone? If not, who else was there? Were any tools/materials used to help them express their views?*

Who is using drugs? (Tick which drugs are used)

Name/relationship to child		Name/relationship to child		Name/relationship to child	
cannabis	☐	cannabis	☐	cannabis	☐
alcohol	☐	alcohol	☐	alcohol	☐
heroin	☐	heroin	☐	heroin	☐
methadone	☐	methadone	☐	methadone	☐
cocaine	☐	cocaine	☐	cocaine	☐
crack	☐	crack	☐	crack	☐
amphetamines	☐	amphetamines	☐	amphetamines	☐
other	☐	other	☐	other	☐

Is this person in treatment for their drug use?

☐ Yes ☐ No	☐ Yes ☐ No	☐ Yes ☐ No

Comment

RESOURCE CASE AUDIT TOOL: CHILD AFFECTED BY PARENTAL ALCOHOL/DRUG MISUSE (page 3)

Evaluation

1. **Content of the assessment**

(a) Is there an informed account of the alcohol/drugs used? Is this information evidence-based?

(b) Has consideration been given to the impact of the alcohol/drug use on the child's developmental needs?

(c) Consideration of alcohol/drug use linked to parenting capacity?

(d) Consideration of alcohol/drug use linked to family and environmental factors?

(e) Has the assessment taken account of previous referrals? Is there a useful chronology?

(f) Does the assessment give you a sense of the child's experiences, hopes and fears?

2. Plan

(a) Does the plan specifically address the issue/impact of parental alcohol/drug use?

(b) Does it set out the outcomes that are to be achieved for the child?

(c) Does it set out the services that will be provided to achieve these outcomes?

(d) Is there a clear process for reviewing outcomes?

3. What happened?

Were plans implemented? Was the child adequately protected and was their welfare promoted?

4. Future action

Is there any action required in relation to:

(a) child/family

(b) staff knowledge and skills

(c) management and supervision

(d) policy and procedures

(e) resources?

Auditors

Signed _____

Date _____

Reviewing multi-agency working

Purpose

To enable multi-agency networks to consider their strategy for meeting the needs of children of alcohol/drug-misusing parents. This could be within single local authorities or localities, or across regions. It is designed to bring key players together to reflect on the strengths and weaknesses of local arrangements, to identify improvements needed, and to develop a plan for achieving these.

Planning the review

It will be important to identify accountability for the review so that any need for action is owned and taken forward. This could be through whatever mechanisms are in place to monitor children's and young people's services' strategic partnerships or local Safeguarding Children boards (LSCB). It is suggested that a special event be convened to undertake the work, but existing meetings could also be used. The process for completing any tasks should be clearly identified and a review process established. Any event will need to be chaired by someone with sufficient authority to ensure that senior people attend and are committed to delivering change. It will also need a facilitator.

Target participants

It will be important to engage senior staff from the following agencies:

- children's social services
- education and early years
- DAAT or their equivalent in a particular area
- substance misuse services
- primary care
- NHS obstetric services
- police
- probation
- the voluntary sector.

Time

One hour.

Process

The chair and others will need to set out the national and local context, including *Hidden Harm*.

PART 1: CURRENT SITUATION

Participants should then complete the following checklist (pages 68–72) within small groups. Each group should be a mix of agencies and professional roles. Each question on the checklist should be considered in turn by the group, and they should try to agree one answer, if possible. It is important that everyone feels free to speak, rather than deferring to the person in the group who is perceived to have the 'right' answer. Evidence for the answer should be recorded: it is not enough to say there is a policy if no-one can identify it.

One person in each group should take responsibility for completing the checklist to represent and record the group's opinion. This should be to a standard where the checklists can be taken away and typed up.

NB: The action boxes at the end of each question *should not* be completed at this stage.

The groups should reconvene into a large group and be given an opportunity to comment on the exercise – whether it was easy/difficult, and any obvious strengths or gaps.

PART 2: WHAT NEEDS TO HAPPEN?

Participants should re-form into their small groups and complete the action boxes on the checklist, identifying the key actions they think need to be undertaken in each area.

Again, one person within the group should take responsibility for recording on the checklist, so that it is legible/understandable for typing.

PART 3: TAKING THE WORK FORWARD

Ask each small group in turn to present its action points on one aspect of the checklist and continue going round the groups until all their action points are identified. Avoid duplication, but identify which points are common across the groups.

These points should be recorded on flip-chart paper.

When the list is complete, invite the group to debate it and to rank the list in order of importance.

FACILITATORS' NOTES

It will be important to consider emerging practice in multi-agency working and facilitators should be aware of work, for example Multi-Agency Working and Information Sharing Project (Home Office 2014). Facilitators may wish to refer to the following at the end of the exercise.

- Is decision making robust?

- Is there duplication of effort?

- Is there improved knowledge management when working together?

- What about the 'borderline' cases – is there risk of them falling through the net?

Getting Our Priorities Right (Scottish Government 2013) has a useful section on Strategic working and multi-agency practice.

It is important to encourage participants to question the evidence if they feel it is inadequate: 'I know we say that's what we do, but do we really?' The discussion within groups may be as important as the conclusions drawn.

Facilitators will need to check on the progress of the exercise to make sure that groups are not getting stuck, or feeling discouraged because they do not have many positive responses.

All the checklists and the flip-charts should be taken away to be typed up, and the process agreed for taking the work forward. It must be clear who is leading on this, and how the work will be incorporated into other plans.

RESOURCE CHILDREN OF ALCOHOL/DRUG-MISUSING PARENTS: REVIEWING MULTI-AGENCY PRACTICE (page 1)

A strategic approach

	Yes	Partly	No	Evidence	Comments
Would you say there was a strategic approach in your local authority to working with families affected by problem drug use?					
Did your local authority develop a plan to consider a response to the *Hidden Harm* report? If so what have been the outcomes?					

Action(s) needed

RESOURCE CHILDREN OF ALCOHOL/DRUG-MISUSING PARENTS: REVIEWING MULTI-AGENCY PRACTICE (page 2)

Case management

Can you identify current guidance for working with the children of alcohol/drug-using parents in your local authority?

	Yes	Partly	No	Evidence	Comments
Identification *Do all services seek to identify families where children (including unborn children) are affected by adult alcohol/drug use?*					
Thresholds for referral *Are the thresholds for making referrals between agencies clear?*					
Information sharing and confidentiality					
Case responsibility					
Ongoing management of concerns about children					
Action(s) needed					

RESOURCE CHILDREN OF ALCOHOL/DRUG-MISUSING PARENTS: REVIEWING MULTI-AGENCY PRACTICE (page 3)

Practice issues

	Yes	Partly	No	Evidence	Comments
Are there any specialist services in your local authority that undertake direct work with children and families affected by parental alcohol/drug misuse?					
Do assessments that take place fully identify the needs of the child?					
Are all the right people contributing to these assessments?					
Action(s) needed					

RESOURCE CHILDREN OF ALCOHOL/DRUG-MISUSING PARENTS: REVIEWING MULTI-AGENCY PRACTICE (page 4)

Staff skills and knowledge

	Yes	Partly	No	Evidence	Comments
Is there specific training in your local authority on working with children of alcohol/drug-misusing parents?					
Do staff working primarily with adults have the skills, knowledge and confidence to identify when children are being affected by parental alcohol/drug misuse?					
Do staff whose primary focus of work is children have the knowledge, skills and confidence to recognise and understand the impact of alcohol/drug misuse on parenting?					
Do foster carers have any dedicated training in looking after, and managing contact for, the children of alcohol/drug-misusing parents?					
Do kinship carers have ongoing support in looking after and managing contact for children of alcohol/ drug-misusing parents?					
Action(s) needed					

General questions

What do you think are the problems with the service provided by agencies, either working individually or jointly, to children of alcohol/drug-misusing parents?

Potential prompts:

How often do staff from agencies consult each other?

Who usually triggers a child protection referral?

Are there joint protocols in place to aid partnership working?

Do the staff involved in adult treatment routinely assess parenting capacity/ability?

What data is collected locally to assist in understanding the needs of children and families affected by alcohol/drug problems in the family?

Any further comments?

3

Training Exercises

Introduction
Purpose

This section of the toolkit contains a series of training exercises and 'sample menus' which trainers may find helpful in putting together courses for a range of participants. The exercises can also be used individually within team training or development sessions. All the original training materials were piloted in the development work with the two local authorities involved in the project. The additional materials are based upon recognised and evaluated programmes from other validated sources. They address different aspects of assessment, decision making and planning for children affected by parental alcohol/drug misuse with a view to enhancing the knowledge and skills of practitioners and managers. Some of the exercises are designed to be delivered within agencies and professional groups: others are designed to be delivered across multi-agency audiences. Target practitioners include:

- children's social workers and managers

- substance misuse workers

- adult care managers with responsibility for substance misuse

- primary care staff

- midwives, obstetric and neonatal staff

- education and early years workers

- foster carers

- fostering and adoption social workers

- child protection coordinators and conference chairs

- independent reviewing officers.

Required skills for trainer(s)

A range of knowledge and skills will be needed to deliver the training. This includes knowledge and/or experience of:

- current systems for assessing children in need, including the Common Assessment Framework, the Framework for the Assessment of Children in Need and Their Families, the Looking After Children system and the Integrated Children's System. Specific knowledge of *Working Together to Safeguard Children* (HM Government 2013, 2015) and the Getting It Right for Every Child approach (Scottish Government) are relevant

- adult alcohol/drug use and drug treatment options

- recent research regarding the impact of parental alcohol/drug misuse on children

- current policy initiatives, including *Hidden Harm*, *Every Child Matters* and *Working Together to Safeguard Children*; and Cafcass (Children and Family Court Advisory Service – England)

- the legal framework for children's services, including the Children Acts 1989 and 2004, the Children's Protection and Adoption Act 2002 and the Children and Young People (Scotland) Act 2014

- children's developmental needs, including the need for secure attachments

- good practice in substitute care for children.

Where trainers do not have all the necessary skills, it may be useful to co-train with others from local agencies, such as substance misuse teams or specialist workers from family placement teams.

Trainers using the resources of this toolkit should be prepared to read and digest all the information given in it and, wherever possible, to use the references to further enhance their knowledge.

Ownership of the training

Training cannot, on its own, bring about changes in practice. It needs to be owned and supported by the agencies from which practitioners are drawn. The involvement of managers at all levels is important so that there can be recognition of the challenges facing front line staff, to enable reflection on any strategic and organisational changes needed to improve practice and to endorse a mandate for such changes. The likelihood of attendance by managers will be improved if the programme is relevant to current local and national issues, such as a review of local procedures or the use of the Common Assessment Framework.

Sensitivity issues

Alcohol and drug use are emotive issues, and can impact on professional or personal lives. It is possible that participants will have had personal experience of both alcohol and drug use, or the experience of others in their immediate family using alcohol or drugs. Training organisations have experienced participants who themselves identify with children's vulnerabilities. Trainers should be aware that this is a potentially emotionally charged subject area, and one that can evoke strong views and feelings from others. Judgemental anecdotes or statements should be challenged and support offered to those whose personal experiences frame the training environment. In their turn, trainers must be offered appropriate support and supervision to undertake this work.

Multidisciplinary training can also create tensions. As well as highlighting perceived differences in status between professional groups and between individuals, misunderstandings can arise through differences in the use of language. Trainers should be aware of the potential for this and seek to clarify or explore the meaning of some terms used – for example, a 'successful treatment outcome' is likely to have different meanings for an adult drugs worker and a child care social worker. There may also be tensions between agencies about referral thresholds or inaccurate ideas about their roles and responsibilities.

These sample menus require considerable preparation and trainers should be prepared to look at all the information contained in this toolkit and make sure that, to the best of their ability, they have all relevant facts at their disposal.

Sample menu 1
Half-day workshop for managers in children's social services
Title

Reflections on practice with the children of alcohol/drug-misusing parents.

Aim

To enable managers to consider best practice, decision making and intervention with the children of problem alcohol and other drug-using parents, and to reflect on current casework.

Target audience

The target audience is a selection of managers within a single local authority:

- senior practitioners with supervisory responsibility for children's social workers

- children's social work team managers

- service managers

- adult social care managers with responsibility for substance misuse services

- child protection coordinators and conference chairs

- independent reviewing officers

- policy and development leads within children's social services.

NB: This course needs to be linked with the one-day course for social workers and social work supervisors (Sample menu 2).

Topic	Activity name	Activity no.
The context: recent policy and research	Adult alcohol and drug problems, children's needs: recent policy and research	2
Consideration of current social work practice in the local authority	Reflecting on practice	12
Obstacles to effective assessment and a proposed multi-agency model	A model for assessment	5
Effective staff supervision	Supervision	14
Ensuring effective practice	Barriers and solutions to effective practice	8

Options

Other materials that could be used include:

- Key messages (pages 30–43)

- Practice tips (pages 44–51)

- Case audit tool (pages 61–64).

It will also be useful to invite managers to bring local issues for discussion if these are likely to have an impact on this area of work, such as relevant serious case reviews or changes in systems/structures.

Sample menu 2
One-day training course for social workers and social work supervisors
Title

Assessing the needs of children with problem alcohol and other drug-using parents.

Aim

To enable participants to understand the effects of alcohol/parental drug misuse on children and to enhance their ability to assess and to meet the needs of children in these circumstances.

Target audience

- children's social workers in assessment/long-term teams
- social work supervisors and managers
- family support workers
- specialist assessment services, for example family centres
- child protection specialists/ conference chairs
- independent reviewing officers.

NB: This course needs to be linked to workshops for managers (Sample menu 1).

Topic	Activity name	Activity no.
Adult alcohol/drug use	Alcohol and drugs quiz	1
The context: recent policy and research	Adult alcohol and drug problems, children's needs: recent policy and research	2
The effects of adult alcohol/drug use on children	Life from a child's perspective	3
Skills in eliciting information from children and parents about alcohol and drugs	Talking about alcohol and drugs: an exercise in interviewing	4
Obstacles to effective assessment and a proposed multi-agency model	A model for assessment	5
Undertaking holistic assessments *or* Assessing the needs of children within legal proceedings	The assessment jigsaw	6
	Specialist assessment exercise	7
Ensuring effective practice	Barriers and solutions to effective practice	8

Options

Other presentations could be developed from materials in the toolkit, depending on the interests of the audience, on:

- Key messages (pages 30–43)

- Practice tips 1, 3 and 4 (pages 44–45, 47, 48–49)

- Caring for the pregnant drug user (pages 156–159)

- Black and minority ethnic drug user (pages 159–161)

- Understanding drugs (pages 161–164).

Sample menu 3
One-day training course for multi-agency practitioners and managers
Title

Working together to meet the needs of the children of problem alcohol and other drug-using parents.

Aim

To enable professionals working with families where there is parental alcohol and/or drug use to understand the possible effects on children and to improve the multi-agency response.

Target audience

- children's social workers and managers

- family support workers

- substance misuse workers

- education and early years staff

- primary care staff

- obstetric and neonatal staff

- voluntary agencies

- family support services.

Topic	Activity name	Activity no.
Adult alcohol/drug use	Alcohol and drugs quiz	1
The context: recent policy and research	Adult alcohol and drug problems, children's needs: recent policy and research	2
The effects of adult alcohol/drug use on children	Life from a child's perspective	3
Skills in eliciting information from children and parents about alcohol and drugs	Talking about alcohol and drugs: an exercise in interviewing	4
Obstacles to effective assessment and a proposed multi-agency model	A model for assessment	5
Multi-agency working	Thresholds for concern	9

Options

Other presentations could be developed from materials in the toolkit, depending on the interests of the audience, on:

- Key messages (pages 30–43)

- Black and minority ethnic drug user (pages 159–161)

- Caring for the pregnant drug user (pages 156–159)

- Understanding drugs (pages 161–164).

Sample menu 4
One-day (short) workshop for foster carers
Title

Caring for the children of problem alcohol and other drug-using parents.

Aim

To consider the concerns and dilemmas faced by foster carers in these circumstances, to share experiences and information and to explore ways of supporting carers to do a good job.

Target audience

- short-term foster carers

- long-term foster carers

- fostering link-workers

- family placement managers.

Topic	Activity name	Activity no.
Adult alcohol/drug use	Alcohol and drugs quiz	1
Effects of adult alcohol and drug use on unborn and newborn children	Presentation on alcohol and drug use in pregnancy	13
The foster care role	Challenges for foster carers	10
Talking to children about alcohol and drugs	Talking about alcohol and drugs: an exercise in interviewing	4
Contact	Contact issues	11

Options

Our experience was that this workshop worked best with short-term foster carers and that the needs of kinship carers and prospective adopters requires a more individualised programme.

Other material in the pack can also be used and/or adapted. This includes:

- Practice tip 5 (pages 50–51)

- A letter from substitute carers (page 43)

- Understanding drugs (pages 161–164)

- A letter from a paediatrician to prospective adopters (pages 176–179).

Activity 1
Alcohol and drugs quiz
Aim

To impart information about the effects of problem alcohol and other drug use.

> **LEARNING OBJECTIVES**
>
> By the end of the session participants will have:
>
> - gained information about a range of drugs that may be misused
>
> - gained information about the effects of alcohol/drug use on behaviour, health and lifestyle
>
> - considered the implications of problem alcohol and other drug use for parenting.

Target audience

The exercise can be used with practitioners and supervisors involved in undertaking assessments of children in need. It can also be used in multi-agency and foster carer training.

Time

One hour.

> **TRAINING MATERIALS/AIDS**
>
> - copies of the Alcohol and drugs quiz – enough for each participant
>
> - copies of the Alcohol and drugs quiz answers – enough for each participant
>
> - copy of the briefing on Understanding drugs (pages 161–164).

Process

1. Ask the participants to divide into pairs or small groups. Explain that this is not an exercise to catch people out or expose how little (or how much) they know about substance use. It is simply a way of imparting information. If there are participants with different levels of knowledge, ensure that groups are mixed.

2. Distribute the quiz to everyone but ask each small group/pair to agree one answer if possible and to appoint someone to record this on the quiz sheet.

3. Go through the answers as a large group, inviting each group/pair to answer in turn. Groups can score one point for each correct answer.

4. There are a number of other drugs which were not referred to in the quiz (e.g. ecstasy, crystal meth, solvents). Ask the group to share what information they know about these drugs or to ask any other questions they may have.

5. Distribute the quiz answer sheets and the briefing on Understanding alcohol and drugs (pages 114–115).

FACILITATORS' NOTES

Trainers might like to suggest that colleagues from the local (adult) substance misuse team assist in facilitating this exercise. Alternatively, if substance misuse workers are participants on the course, invite them to contribute their knowledge during stages 3 and 4.

This could also be an opportunity to give information about local resources and routes of referral to these resources. Written information about contact details would also be useful. The DrugScope website, which since the demise of DrugScope in 2015 is now a legacy website, provides information about drugs and their effects: www.drugscope.org.uk. It may be helpful to get local information from the police in a given area.

NB: Be mindful that drug use is an emotive issue and participants may have strong views or personal experiences that may make the exercise difficult for them.

RESOURCE ALCOHOL AND DRUGS QUIZ (page 1)

Alcohol

1. Alcohol is a drug. *True or False?*

2. Alcohol is… *Choose from the following:*

    (a) a stimulant?   (b) a depressant?   (c) neither?

3. Alcohol affects mental judgement before physical coordination. *True or False?*

4. Daily drinking indicates someone has an alcohol problem. *True or False?*

5. Which of these would make you worry about someone's drinking levels?

    (a) high tolerance

    (b) depression and isolation

    (c) loss of interest in food/hygiene/surroundings?

Amphetamines

1. Can you name two slang names given to amphetamine sulphate?

    . . . .

2. After the effects of amphetamine use have worn off, which of these symptoms might a user feel?

    (a) tired and lethargic

    (b) hungry

    (c) irritable and aggressive

    (d) depressed

Cannabis

1. Does regular cannabis use lead to physical dependence?

    . . . .

2. In January 2004 the law relating to cannabis was amended and in 2009 it was reclassified again. Is it legal to possess cannabis (for personal use only) and to smoke cannabis in public places?

    . . . .

3. Is it possible to overdose on cannabis?

    . . . .

4. What is skunk?

    . . . .

RESOURCE ALCOHOL AND DRUGS QUIZ (page 2)

Cocaine/crack

1. What is crack?

    . . . .

2. How much does a rock of crack cost in your area?

    . . . .

3. What is a speedball?

    (a) an alcoholic drink made with raw eggs

    (b) a combination of Prozac and alcohol

    (c) a form of crack cocaine that is swallowed

    (d) a combination of crack and heroin

4. A few tries of crack and you're addicted. Is this statement true or false?

    . . . .

Benzodiazepines (tranquillisers)

1. Benzodiazepines are prescribed to:

    (a) relieve anxiety

    (b) combat insomnia

    (c) reduce problem alcohol use

    (d) suppress appetite

2. Are benzodiazepines addictive?

    . . . .

RESOURCE ALCOHOL AND DRUGS QUIZ (page 3)

Heroin

1. The symptoms of sudden withdrawal from long-term heroin use are most similar to which of the following?

   (a) epileptic fit

   (b) heart attack

   (c) influenza

   (d) migraine attack

   (e) malaria

2. How pure is the average heroin sold on the street?

   . . . .

3. Which of these are prescribed as substitutes for heroin use?

   (a) Subutex

   (b) Neurofen

   (c) benzodiazepines

   (d) methadone

4. Heroin kills more people than any other drug in the UK. *True or False?*

   . . . .

5. Which of the following would a first-time heroin user be most likely to experience?

   (a) vomiting

   (b) instant addiction

   (c) a feeling of drowsiness and warmth

RESOURCE ALCOHOL AND DRUGS QUIZ (page 4)

Other drugs

1. What is ketamine?

    (a) a veterinary anaesthetic

    (b) a very strong form of cannabis

    (c) another name for an ecstasy tablet

2. What are 'legal highs'?

3. If someone presented with the following behaviours or indicators, what drugs might they have taken?

Effect	Possible cause
extreme drowsiness; inability to stay awake	
euphoria, disinhibition and talkativeness	
restlessness and anxiety	
paranoia and aggression	
lack of appetite	
abscesses	

★

RESOURCE ALCOHOL AND DRUGS
QUIZ: ANSWERS (page 1)

Alcohol

1. Alcohol is a drug.

   True.

2. Alcohol is... *Choose from the following:*

   (a) a stimulant?   (b) a depressant?   (c) neither?

   Alcohol is a depressant, although it may feel like a stimulant.

3. Alcohol affects mental judgement before physical coordination.

   True.

4. Daily drinking indicates someone has an alcohol problem.

   False; but if there are other factors then it could be true.

5. Which of these would make you worry about someone's drinking levels?

   (a) high tolerance

   (b) depression and isolation

   (c) loss of interest in food/hygiene/surroundings?

   All of these are warning signs that someone has a problem with alcohol.

Amphetamines

1. Can you name two slang names given to amphetamine sulphate?

   Amphetamine sulphate is also known as speed, billy, whizz, sulphate. It is also available in a more concentrated crystal form called 'ice' or crystal meth. Amphetamines are one of the most commonly available illegal drugs. Although they are very cheap, they are often of very low purity (sometimes 5 per cent pure or less), and this is dangerous when amphetamines are injected.

2. After the effects of amphetamine use have worn off, which of these symptoms might a user feel?

   (a) tired and lethargic

   (b) hungry

   (c) irritable and aggressive

   (d) depressed

   All are correct. After the effects of amphetamine use have worn off a user might experience any or all of these symptoms. Extreme tiredness, hunger, depression and feeling lethargic are common.

Some users describe the effect as being like 'borrowed energy' that wears off. After a long period of use, users tend to need a long sleep to recover.

Cannabis

1. Does regular cannabis use lead to physical dependence?

    No. Cannabis does not produce physical dependence, though regular users may develop a strong psychological need for the drug and a reliance on it in social situations.

2. In January 2004 the law relating to cannabis was amended and in 2009 it was reclassified. Is it legal to possess cannabis (for personal use only) and to smoke cannabis in public places?

    The reclassification of cannabis is confusing. The possession and supply of cannabis is a criminal offence. The drug was reclassified (from Class B to Class C) in 2004 which affected the penalties for those charged with possession. In 2009 cannabis was reclassified again back to a Class B drug, with corresponding penalties.

3. Is it possible to overdose on cannabis?

    No. Consuming large amounts in a short space of time may lead users to become disorientated and dizzy, and they may vomit. Greater dangers are posed by the mental health effects and the increased risk of cancer. Three to four joints a day are thought to cause as much bronchial damage as 20 cigarettes. Regular cannabis use can impair concentration and short-term memory. There is some evidence, albeit conflicting, about cannabis use and mental health difficulties.

4. What is skunk?

    Skunk is a hybrid (genetically engineered) form of cannabis which is very strong, and produces an effect more intense than that of normal cannabis.

Cocaine/crack

1. What is crack?

   This is a purer form of cocaine produced by a chemical process – most commonly done by cooking it with baking powder in a microwave. This leaves pure crystalline cocaine, which is broken into chunks (rocks) and sold in small wraps of cling film or silver foil. It produces a crackling sound when burned – hence the name. Crack burns easily and is usually smoked in pipes – sometimes made from bottles or soft drinks cans – or else it can be mixed with tobacco or cannabis or burned on tinfoil. It can also be injected after being made soluble.

2. How much does a rock of crack cost in your area?

   The price of all drugs is affected by supply and demand. Crack tends to be cheaper in large urban areas, where it is more readily available.

3. What is a speedball?

   (a) an alcoholic drink made with raw eggs

   (b) a combination of Prozac and alcohol

   (c) a form of crack cocaine that is swallowed

   (d) a combination of crack and heroin

   (d) is correct – a combination of crack and heroin, often injected. It is also known as a snowball. Taken together, the effects of the two drugs are enhanced – as are the risks: heart attack and overdose. Heroin can be used as a 'comedown' from crack, and sometimes crack users develop a heroin habit this way.

4. A few tries of crack and you're addicted. Is this statement true or false?

   False. Cocaine and crack cocaine are not physically addictive, and stopping use will not produce physical withdrawal symptoms. But it is psychologically very addictive. Crack cocaine produces a very intense, short-lived and pleasurable experience which users wish to repeat. The powerful compulsion to repeat this experience can lead to users going on a binge, and heavy use can be very difficult to control. After-effects of use can be unpleasant, and include tiredness, depression and intense irritability.

★

Benzodiazepine (tranquillisers)

1. Benzodiazepines are prescribed to:

   (a) relieve anxiety

   (b) combat insomnia

   (c) reduce problem alcohol use

   (d) suppress appetite

   (a) and (b) are correct. Benzodiazepines are usually prescribed to relieve anxiety and to combat insomnia. They are the most commonly prescribed tranquillisers, and include brand names such as Valium (diazepam), Librium and Ativan. Many poly-drug users will use benzodiazepines when their drug of choice is unavailable.

2. Are benzodiazepines addictive?

   Yes. There is a very high risk of dependency, and benzodiazepines are as physically addictive as opiates, with equivalent difficulty in stopping their use. Withdrawal should be done under medical supervision, and symptoms can include headaches, blurred or double vision, insomnia and nightmares, fits and rashes. Babies exposed antenatally will also have withdrawal symptoms.

RESOURCE ALCOHOL AND DRUGS
QUIZ: ANSWERS (page 3)

Heroin

1. The symptoms of sudden withdrawal from long-term heroin use are most similar to which of the following:

   (a) epileptic fit

   (b) heart attack

   (c) influenza

   (d) migraine attack

   (e) malaria

   (c) influenza. The withdrawal effects vary from person to person, but are most often experienced as a bad dose of influenza and a craving for the drug. Aching limbs, restlessness, sweating and diarrhoea and vomiting can also occur. In most cases the symptoms will disappear after two to three weeks. Staying off is more difficult than stopping.

2. How pure is the average heroin sold on the street?

   Evidence is different from location to location. In some areas, at some times, heroin may be very pure and may cause overdose and death in substantial numbers. Most heroin powder has been adulterated with a variety of powders of similar appearance, such as chalk dust, glucose powder, caffeine, flour and talcum powder.

3. Which of these are prescribed as opiate substitutes?

   (a) Subutex

   (b) Nurofen

   (c) benzodiazepines

   (d) methadone

   (a) Subutex and (d) methadone are the two most common substitute prescriptions. Subutex is dissolved under the tongue and less toxic than methadone, so less dangerous if taken accidentally. It also acts as a blocker to the effects of heroin, and so reduces the desire for people to use on top. Methadone is usually prescribed as a linctus. The effects of methadone are long-lasting (24 hours) and act to prevent withdrawal symptoms. Diamorphine (heroin) can be prescribed, though this is unusual and requires a Home Office licence. Dihydrocodeine (also known as DF118) is also used as an opiate substitute.

4. Heroin kills more people than any other drug in the UK. *True or False?*

   False. Nicotine causes over 100,000 deaths annually (through cancers, heart disease and chest infection). There were 8697 alcohol-related deaths registered in the UK in 2014 (Office for National Statistics 2016). Heroin causes about 250 deaths a year. This figure fluctuates each year.

5. Which of the following would a first-time heroin user be most likely to experience?

(a) vomiting

(b) instant addiction

(c) a feeling of drowsiness and warmth.

(a) vomiting and (c) drowsiness and warmth. First-time use is usually accompanied by vomiting. Opiates induce a relaxed detachment from pain and anxiety, and users describe this as a feeling of warmth, contentment and drowsiness. Addiction or physical dependence builds up gradually, and will depend on the amount and frequency of use.

RESOURCE ALCOHOL AND DRUGS
QUIZ: ANSWERS (page 4)

Other drugs

1. What is ketamine?

    (a) a veterinary anaesthetic

    (b) a very strong form of cannabis

    (c) another name for an ecstasy tablet

    Ketamine was originally used as an anaesthetic for animals. It can produce mild hallucinations and a feeling of euphoria. It is also called Special K.

2. What are 'legal highs'?

    Legal highs are substances that have similar effects to illegal drugs like cocaine or cannabis. They are sometimes called more accurately new psychoactive substances (NPS) or 'club drugs'. Many of these drugs are now controlled, but some are still legal to possess. This does not mean that they are safe or approved for people to use. They can carry serious health risks.

3. If someone presented with the following behaviours or indicators, what drugs might they have taken?

Effect	Possible cause
extreme drowsiness; inability to stay awake	opiates (heroin or methadone); benzodiazepines; cannabis; ketamine
euphoria, disinhibition and talkativeness	ecstasy; cocaine; crack; amphetamines; cannabis; alcohol
restlessness and anxiety	cocaine; crack cocaine; amphetamines; opiate withdrawal
paranoia and aggression	after-effects of stimulant use
lack of appetite	stimulants, especially amphetamines and cocaine intravenous; alcohol
abscesses	drug use

Further information about a wide range of drugs and their effects can be found on the following websites:

- DrugWise: www.drugwise.org.uk

- FRANK: www.talktofrank.com

- National Treatment Agency: www.nta.nhs.uk (NTA is now part of Public Health England but retains its own dedicated website).

Activity 2
Adult alcohol and drug problems, children's needs: recent policy and research
Aim

To describe the policy and research context which highlights the importance of work with the children of problem alcohol/drug users.

LEARNING OBJECTIVES

By the end of the session participants will have:

- considered key policy initiatives

- heard about recent research highlighting the perspectives of key stakeholders

- considered the implications for their practice.

Target audience

This exercise can be used with practitioners and supervisors involved in undertaking assessments of children in need. It can also be used in multi-agency training.

Time

Sixty minutes.

TRAINING MATERIALS/AIDS

- PowerPoint presentation, available to download from the JKP website.

Process

Presentation by the facilitator, using the following slides, then a short group discussion.

Options: alternative presentations could be developed based on other materials in the toolkit from the Key messages section.

PowerPoint: Adult alcohol and drug problems, children's needs: recent policy and research

---

Why do we need to focus on the needs of children with drug and/ or alcohol-misusing parents?

- *Hidden Harm*

- *Hidden Harm Three Years On* (Advisory Council on the Misuse of Drugs 2007)

- Working Together to Safeguard Children agenda

    - outcomes focused

    - need for integration

    - common assessment

continued

---

continued

- Learning Lessons from Serious Case Reviews (Ofsted 2009–10)

- Joint Guidance on Development of Local Protocols between Drug and Alcohol Treatment Services and Local Safeguarding and Family Service (DCSF, DoH and NTA 2009)

- New estimates of the number of children living with substance-misusing parents: results from UK national household surveys (Manning *et al.* 2009)

- *Medications in Drug Treatment: Tackling the Risks to Children* (ADFAM 2014 and Year + 1 Report, ADFAM 2015)

- *Silent Voices* (Adamson and Templeton 2012)

- One million children affected by alcohol problems of parents (Forrester 2012)

Hidden Harm

- 250,000–350,000 children living with drug-using parents (2013)
- Causes serious harm from conception to adulthood
- Reducing harm should be priority
- Joint working can protect and improve children's health and wellbeing
- Number will only decrease as drug use decreases
- 61,928 adults in drug treatment with parental responsibility
- 55% of people in treatment are either parents or have children living with them)

Recommendations for social care

- Integrated approach, based on common assessment
- Training on alcohol/drugs/impact on children – basic + PQ
- Coordinated resources – to assist parents and protect children
- Improved support to children – day fostering, one-to-one and group work support, trained kinship/foster carers
- Rapid evidence-based decisions about permanence
- Child protection policies to take account of alcohol/drug-using parents

What do the children say?

- *Parental Drug and Alcohol Misuse* – young people 15–27
    - violence and neglect
    - had to 'manage the knowledge'
    - parents cared 'about' them but couldn't care 'for' them
    - alcohol = violence; drugs = fear + secrecy
    - had to find survival strategies
    - support from others 'conditional'
    - passage to adulthood disrupted and many were misusing substances themselves

Bancroft *et al.* (2004) and more recent research, e.g. Houmoller *et al.* (2011)

What else do children say?

- *Understanding What Children Say about Living with Domestic Violence, Parental Substance Misuse or Parental Health Problems*
    - children more aware – and more worried – than is recognised
    - do not know where to get formal help
    - worried that professionals won't talk to them, won't believe them or won't act
    - want information to help them understand
    - ...and someone to talk to who can be trusted

Gorin (2004)

Emotional impact on child's development

- Living with an elephant: growing up with parental substance misuse

    ○ household revolves around substance misuse but no-one talks about it

    ○ child can't trust own perceptions – is it me?

    ○ leads to confusion and grief

    ○ poor attachment and self-esteem

Kroll (2004)

- Children who say the least are of the most concern

Hill et al. (2011b)

What do families say?

- Between a rock and a hard place: the role of protecting children from the effects of parental drug problems

    ○ substantial numbers of relatives have taken on caring role – usually informally

    ○ but not without its problems...

        - inconsistency – fluctuates with drug use

        - monitoring element

        - diminished parenthood

        - perpetuating the drug use?

Barnard (2003)

What else do families say?

- *Drugs in the Family: The Impact on Parents and Siblings*
    - family try to sort it out on their own
    - has effect on parents' own health
    - conflict as drug user's needs take over
    - siblings miss the relationship they had
    - anger, shame and loss
    - younger children also begin using – sometimes deliberately introduced

Barnard (2005)

Impact – alcohol

- Disruption to family life – but web of social and environmental factors/child's specific age development
- Child protection issues
- Gender and parenting – consider:
    - mothers – shame, guilt, conflict over marital and parental roles (Kahler *et al.* 2003)
    - exposure to violence
    - fathers – heightened sensitivity and lower tolerance to behaviour and needs of infant children (Eiden and Leonard 2000)

'Parental alcohol misuse damages and disrupts the lives of children and families in all areas of society spanning all social classes; it blights the lives of whole families and harms the developing children trapped by the effects of their parents' problematic drinking.' (Turning Point 2006, *Bottling It Up*)

Possible harm

- Being drunk more often

- Taking day off for hangover

- Accidents, rows and injuries due to drink

- Getting into trouble due to drink

- Doing something that you wouldn't do normally and regretting it

- Drinking more than you planned

Probable harm

- Obsessive thinking

- Gulping first drink

- Being first to finish

- Needing, not choosing a drink

- Spending more than you can afford

- Secret drinking

- Hiding drink evidence

- People telling you they are worried

Definition of dependence

- Sense of compulsion

- Impaired capacity to control use and amount

- Withdrawal states (nausea, shakes, etc.)

- Tolerance

- Preoccupation with alcohol

- Use despite harm

What is it about alcohol?

- Tolerant and accepting social attitudes towards alcohol

- Need for real understanding of the impact – research and evidence-based practice requirements

- Patterns of use of alcohol and impact are changing

continued

continued

- Legality

- Perspectives (of others)

- Attitudes of society

- Attitudes and approach of services

- Costs and availability

- Coverage of media

- Less visibility of children

- Types of drink

- Alcohol and links to domestic violence

- More varied social-economic status

- Alcohol a greater cost

Aberlour Child Care Trust Think Tank Report
A Matter of Substance? Alcohol or Drugs (2007)

Parenting impact on children

- Emotional unavailability and inconsistency

- Unpredictable behaviour

- Social exclusion

- Child as ally/protector/carer

- Don't talk, don't trust, don't feel

continued

continued

- Poor school achievement (Velleman and Orford 1999)

- Behavioural difficulties – lack of concentration

- Low self-esteem and emotional problems

- Family disruption – violence

- Precocious maturity

- Self blame

- Long-term effect into adulthood

continued

---

continued

- High levels of family disharmony

- Domestic violence

- Physical, sexual or emotional abuse

- Inconsistent, ambivalent or neglectful parenting

- Parental loss

- Material deprivation and neglect

- Dealing with denial

(Forrester 2004; Velleman and Templeton 2007)

Research into social work response

- 'Social work and parental substance misuse'
  - most common problem for social workers
  - inter-agency work/referrals were rare
  - social workers poorly prepared
  - alcohol associated with young children/CPR
  - drug use with babies/care proceedings
  - 2 years from referral 54% no longer at home
  - are we under-reacting to chronic concerns?

  Forrester and Harwin (2004)

What are the implications for assessment and decision making?

- Tackling denial and secrecy
- Seeing life from the child's point of view
- Need to understand substance use
- Recognising the importance of extended family
- Skills in direct work with children
- Identifying disguised compliance
- Working with resistant families
- Attitudes and values – professional and personal
- Autonomous professional judgement

Activity 3
Life from a child's perspective
Aim

To enable participants to consider the experiences of children living with parents who are alcohol/drug users, and to help professionals undertake assessments from the perspective of the needs of the child.

LEARNING OBJECTIVES

By the end of the session participants will have:

- considered how children feel in situations where family life is affected by parental alcohol/drug use

- gained an insight into a child's interpretation of their needs

- explored a professional's perception of children's needs.

Target audience

This exercise can be used with practitioners and supervisors involved in undertaking assessments of children in need. It can also be used in multi-agency training.

Time

Three hours.

TRAINING MATERIALS/AIDS

- copies of the two case scenarios, Maria's story and Mandy's story – enough for each participant

- PowerPoint presentation, available to download from the JKP website

- paper and pens (you could prepare them as a diary page)

- flip-charts and pens

- copies of Applying the Assessment Framework (page 53).

Process
PART 1

Introduce the exercise by talking about the fact that assessments of children whose parents are problem alcohol and/or drug users can present particular difficulties because of the hidden and illegal nature of the problem in the case of drugs and societal tolerance in the case of alcohol. Both parents and children can minimise the impact to practitioners and assessments may not consider the perspective of the child – how they experience life at home or at school. It is important that all practitioners focus on the child and their needs, and that assessments are not dominated by parental crises. An understanding of the experience of a child who lives with a parent who uses drugs and alcohol to excess will make any assessment more meaningful and inform an analysis of their needs. Show the PowerPoint presentation to hear the voices of real children and reflect upon their expectations from their parents as they grow.

1. Ask the group to divide into (at least three) smaller groups. Give each participant a copy of the case scenario, Maria's story, and ask them to spend five minutes reading through it. Each group should then choose or be assigned a different child from the scenario given and, together, consider what life would feel like from this child's point of view. The group should then write an imaginary diary for 'A day in the life of…' The diary must be written in the first person, and the group will need to decide who will write it down on the group's behalf.

2. Do the same with Mandy's story.

3. Bring the small groups together, taking care to de-role where necessary. Ask for feedback about how it felt to be in the position of this child. What sort of emotions did this evoke? What do they think the child would have wanted from professionals involved? What might the differences be between Maria's children and Mandy's children? How would you deal with these cases? Ask for a volunteer to read out the diary from each of the smaller groups.

PART 2

4. Returning to the original smaller groups, give each participant a copy of the diagram Applying the Assessment Framework (page 53). Thinking of their child, ask the groups to identify the particular areas of relevance. What aspects would you be most concerned about? (What information would you want to find out, and who would you ask?)

5. Bring the groups together and take general feedback of the main learning points for them all.

FACILITATORS' NOTES

This exercise can provoke strong feelings. It is important that participants are supported to stick with these feelings and to express them safely. The facilitator may need to remind participants to stay in the first person when writing the diary, and to discourage them from hiding behind professional roles.

What we may expect from our parents

- Parents/care givers – centre of our world as children
- They help us to understand and make sense of the world
- Security, reassurance; certainty; development of self; value of others; confidence; empathy

Children's voices
Responsibility

'I used to feel responsible but then I realised it wasn't my fault, she didn't love me enough, or she would have stopped (drinking) before.'

(Lorne aged 12 – Turning Point 2006)

Finding another way

'I just had to decide myself that even though I loved my mum and cared a lot about her…I wanted to live on my own. Still go to visit her and at least if I went to see her and if it got out of hand and she got too drunk and violent I could walk away.'

(Girl aged 18 – Dearden and Becker 2000)

Desperation
Sangeeta aged 13 – reported at 3pm and told Childline:

'My mum left home around 6pm last night after having an argument. She is not back yet. She has done this before. I am feeling scared, lonely and hungry. I can stay with Dad, but he is an alcoholic. I saw him last a couple of months ago.'

Not being there

'I was looking out for them 'cos they said they would come but they never... I thought they must no' care about me then...things like racing, yer school sports, and they said they would come but they never...when I think about it now, it was like heart breaking, it wasn't very nice...'

(Susan aged 14 – Barnard and Barlow 2003)

Lifting the veil

'He always shuts the door if he was using, but it was not something you can ever, I think, like 100% when you're living in the same house, as some one because you just know, you just know.'

(Dena aged 17 – Houmoller *et al.* 2011)

Role reversal, role confusion and the child as carer

'Dear Mommy,

Don't worry, I went out to play, I let you sleep... Harry will be in the yard and I will be at Joanne's or Mary Ann's. Harry wore a sweatshirt and play jacket with just the hood on his ears. I wore my red pants with my red and white hat with a hood.'

(Linda aged 8 – Seval Brooks and Rice in Recovery 1997)

The hurt that words engender

'[He] roars at me and calls me a scumbag and other bad words that hurt my feelings.'

(Boy aged 11 – ISPCC 2011)

Separating the personal and public life

'They (mates) didn't know cause they were like wallies, and they'd like, wind me up about it…if I told my mates, my mates would tell the bullies, and like they would say, oh, like "is Mummy not looking after you properly?"'

(Ben aged 10 – Houmoller *et al.* 2011)

RESOURCE MARIA'S STORY

Maria is a single mother with three children: Stefan aged 13, Kylie aged 9 and Jake aged 15 months. The family have been placed in temporary accommodation following a fire at their flat. The children have different fathers, and the current partner, Mike, is a crack dealer and violent towards her. All the family are white UK in origin, and Maria's parents used to live nearby but have recently retired to Spain. Professionals find Maria difficult to engage; sometimes she is chatty and friendly but other times she can be hostile and abusive. She is known to have smoked cocaine heavily in the past. She has several convictions for prostitution and shoplifting, and has some outstanding offences for which she may receive a custodial sentence. The Probation Service has been asked to prepare a pre-sentence report, and Maria tells the probation officer the following:

I was really unlucky to get nicked this time – hadn't been working Kings Cross for months, but needed to get money quickly to buy things for the kids. I like them to look good – Stefan wanted some trainers for £100 and Kylie needs a leather jacket. Mike is back on the scene and never pays a penny towards anything – still, it's better than being on my own with the kids. It's driving me mad being cooped up in that hostel with them all day. He's been as nice as pie and promises there'll be no more violence. I admit we have used a bit of crack – his mates keep bringing it round – but we can handle it. The biggest problem is the next morning – you feel so rough it's hard to get going. Of course the kids don't know – what sort of mother do you think I am? The kids are fine. Kylie's a real little mother to Jake – the other day I even found her making him a bottle. She looks after him if I have to pop out. Stefan's getting a bit stroppy – he was brought home by a neighbour at midnight the other day, and she said he'd been chucking bricks over the balcony and we should have been watching him. Mike soon told her where to get off. Jake's OK but into everything. My mum used to have him a lot but she's not around now. They gave me a nursery place, but the woman in charge was always moaning if I was a bit late collecting him – and she started to say things about him being miserable. It was more trouble than it was worth, so I don't go now. School? The kids are OK I suppose. We did get a letter about Stefan bunking off, but then all kids do that, don't they? Kylie loves school – gets herself up and out now. She's disappointed that I took Mike back – she's worse than my mum when it comes to bossing me about. Anyway, what are you going to put in that report then? There's no-one to look after them if I go inside – Kylie and Stefan are really worried about it.

Your task

1. Looking at Maria's story, imagine you are one of her children.

2. Write a brief diary of an imaginary day. What happens at school/home?

3. In your diary, describe how you experience your day – and stick to the first person (I, not s/he).

4. Choose a person in the group to record the diary on behalf of the group.

RESOURCE MANDY'S STORY

My name is Mandy.

I like living in (insert local area), as much as anything because I'm away from my family. I love them but I can't be around them, they're all over my sister but I've never quite made it in their eyes. She's a housing support worker and they can't do enough to help her out, looking after her kids so she can work.

Me, they don't like me because I won't play their games, you know, pretending everything is happy families. My dad always pushed me around. That's all I can say really. I have to keep the rest to myself or I'd lose it.

Then, you know what, my bloke turned out just like my dad – a bully who never did a stroke. We came here 'cos he said he had friends here, and he got us evicted from our last place for non-payment of rent. Seemed like a bit of a laugh at the time, but when we got here, I found out I was pregnant. He was really angry about it, put me in hospital with a broken pelvis. God knows how the baby survived, but it did. He left me just about as soon as Stephen was born. Can't take responsibility. Some men. He came back for a while, got me pregnant again then off he goes! I don't miss him really, but I've been left with debts and coping with both kids on my own the last four years. If it weren't for some friends in the pub I would have gone under.

The worst is being on my own all the time with Stephen and Sam, he's nearly six. One or two drinks in the evening help me feel better in myself, not so frightened. And then I can relax. Sometimes I pop out for a quick drink, only when the kids are asleep though. It's not like I can't do without a drink, but I wouldn't want to. It's my only pleasure, and anyway, I play a lot more with the kids when I'm a bit merry, so they love it.

I shout a lot sometimes when I'm tired, but underneath I'm a big softy. Stephen and Sam know that. They know I love them. They're fine with me, accept me as I am. I'm not saying I'm the best mum in the world but they're OK. I'm a lot more loving than my mam was! Stephen seems to manage fine on his own anyway, he's my little helper. You'd never believe he was only eight, acts right grown up! Always fussing round Sam, like a little daddy! He has a really quizzical look on his face sometimes, makes me laugh he does.

Problem is, I met the kids' gran at the school the other day, I was a bit merry, and now I think the school will have been in touch with 'the authorities' – don't know what will happen next!??

(Adapted from *Alcohol and Parenting*, Alcohol Concern 2009)

Your task

1. Looking at Mandy's story, imagine you are one of her children.

2. Write a brief diary of an imaginary day. What happens at school/home?

3. In your diary, describe how you experience your day – and stick to the first person (I, not s/he).

4. Choose a person in the group to record the diary on behalf of the group.

Activity 4
Talking about alcohol and drugs: an exercise in interviewing
Aim

To enable participants to practise interviewing adult alcohol/drug users and/or to practise talking to children affected by parental problem alcohol and other drug use.

LEARNING OBJECTIVES

By the end of the session participants will have:

- considered how children might feel when asked to talk about the impact on them of drug and alcohol use by their parents

- considered how adults might feel when asked about their alcohol and/or drug use

- gained insight into the form of questions that would facilitate information gathering.

Target audience

This exercise can be used with practitioners and supervisors involved in undertaking assessments of children in need. It can also be used on inter-agency training courses. It is also suitable for very large audiences, and could be adapted for use, for example, at a conference. Finally, it could be used on foster carer training courses.

Time

Thirty minutes.

TRAINING MATERIALS/AIDS

- pre-prepared flip-charts, each containing one of the suggested scenarios. These could also be prepared on a PowerPoint slide. They must not be visible to participants until permission is given – see below

- copies of the diagram Applying the Assessment Framework (page 53).

Introduction to the exercise

Explain the assessment diagram by saying that it is an aid to thinking about the particular issues that may be relevant in families where parents use drugs and/or alcohol. This could be something that affects parenting capacity, such as the need to spend benefits on their drug of choice rather than food, or on the child's developmental needs, such as a feeling of being less important than drugs or alcohol.

Communicating with children in these circumstances can often be very difficult. It may be there is a culture of denial and secrecy in the family. Children can become embarrassed and frightened, and quite mistrustful. The idea of 'the elephant in the living room' is quite helpful – an enormous but secret presence that takes up the family's space, time and attention, and a presence that nobody talks about.

It can be equally difficult for adults to talk about a part of their lives that is illegal. Or in the case of alcohol, that which is embarrassing and societally unacceptable and normally done in private. Denial and minimisation will be common. There is likely to be enormous fear about the possible repercussions of disclosure of substance use and a fear that children will be automatically removed.

Process

Choose which scenario is to be used for the exercise and ask participants to get into pairs and allocate roles. These are either as professional (interviewer) or adult/child (interviewee).

- For scenario 1 the roles will need to be that of an adult drug user and a professional.

- For scenario 2 the roles will need to be that of a nine-year-old boy and a professional.

- For scenario 3 the roles will need to be that of an eight-year-old girl and a foster carer.

- For scenario 4 the roles will need to be that of an adult alcohol user and a professional.

1. Ask the 'professionals' to close their eyes.

2. Uncover the background details on the flip-chart (or show the PowerPoint slide).

3. Those playing the role of the adult/child interviewee will then be asked to read these brief details. Once they are familiar with them, the facilitator should cover over the details.

4. The professionals now have ten minutes to talk to their adult or child and to elicit information from them about one dimension of the assessment diagram.

   - For scenarios 1 and 4, this will be the parent's capacity to protect the child from the impact of their substance use.

   - For scenario 2, this will be the quality of the attachment and the extent to which the child feels valued at home.

   - For scenario 3, this will be the extent to which the child feels stigmatised because of her parent's drug use, and whether she has any related concerns.

5. The person being interviewed shouldn't lie if asked a direct question, but doesn't have to volunteer information otherwise – unless they want to.

6. Return to the large group and ask participants to describe how this exercise felt. What did the professionals feel? What sort of difficulties did they experience? For the adults and children being interviewed, how did it feel to be in this role? What questions helped and what got in the way of giving information?

7. End the exercise by uncovering the flip-chart and showing the group what they were supposed to be finding out.

RESOURCE TALKING ABOUT SUBSTANCES: AN EXERCISE IN INTERVIEWING

Scenario 1

You are an injecting heroin user spending about £30 a day. You sometimes buy methadone when you can't get heroin. You have two children, aged 20 months and six years. You keep the methadone in the kitchen fridge and the heroin hidden in the bedroom. You never inject in front of the children, and try to do so in the mornings or the evenings when they're asleep.

Scenario 2

You are a nine-year-old boy, very upset at school. Your parents are both drug users, although no-one talks about it. They think you don't know, but you do. It's your birthday today, and you had been promised a PlayStation and a birthday party. You told everyone at school and they're asking you about it. This morning there was no present and no party planned. They had forgotten. You wish you had normal parents.

Scenario 3

You are an eight-year-old girl, looked after by foster carers. You have been told that your mother is ill and has had to go to hospital. Today other children at school told you your mum is a 'smackhead' and a 'druggie'. You have had drug education at school and know drugs are wrong. You are worried she will die or go to prison.

Scenario 4

You are a 34-year-old female recruitment consultant with three children aged ten, eight and six. You care for the children most of the time on your own as your partner is away a lot on business. You drink recreationally with family and friends, but top up when no-one is looking. When you are alone you drink frequently and can get through a bottle of wine a night. You have a very demanding job.

Activity 5
A model for assessment
Aim

To introduce participants to a model for undertaking holistic assessments of the needs of children affected by parental problem alcohol and other drug use.

LEARNING OBJECTIVES

By the end of the session participants will be:

- aware of the challenges and pitfalls in undertaking such assessments

- familiar with a model Applying the Assessment Framework in such circumstances

- introduced to the method for involving all agencies in assessment.

Target audience

This exercise can be used with practitioners and supervisors involved in undertaking assessments of children in need, or with multi-agency audiences.

Time

Twenty minutes.

TRAINING MATERIALS/AIDS

- PowerPoint presentation, available to download from the JKP website

- copies of the Assessment Model (pages 51–59).

Process

Presentation by the facilitator, followed by large group discussion.

Options

Facilitator may develop an alternative presentation using local data or other material in the toolkit.

Nature of the workload

- Little specific guidance *but*:

    - children of drug-misusing parents may account for about 20% of CPR and 15% of looked after children. Areas of the country will differ

    - many children not with mothers/parents – with little prospect of return home

    - families have multiple problems – not 'just' drugs

    - some large families, with multi-generational use

Challenges for assessment

- Recognition and engagement

    - inconsistent thresholds for referral

    - avoidant workers and families?

    - disguised compliance

- Possible problems with quality?

    - repeated initial assessments

    - single agency not joint effort

    - crisis led not proactive

    - lack of knowledge re substances/impact on children

    - fathers often omitted

    - ...as are wider family/networks

    - children may be invisible

More practice messages

- Partnership working
    - under-developed – with other agencies
    - ...and children/families themselves
    - little use of FGCs/network meetings?
- Decision making
    - impeded by bureaucracy
    - lack of analysis?
    - naivety about drugs and alcohol use – too much emphasis on parental abstinence not children's needs?
    - lack of experience of working with more affluent and articulate individuals
    - residential assessments – purposeful or a safe place to fail?

Care planning

- Entry at point of no return
    - accident not design?
- Inconsistent use of kinship care
    - poor recognition of conflicting loyalties
    - need for clear expectations/support
- Rehabilitation...or not?
    - one more change...but is it likely to succeed?
    - the importance of history
    - can the child wait?
    - need for contingency/parallel/concurrent planning

Applying the Assessment Framework

- effect of prenatal exposure to drugs
- subsequent special health needs as a result of above
- access or exposure to drugs/equipment
- effect on school attendance and ability to learn
- impact on quality of attachment(s) and feeling valued
- attitudes to drug use and offending behaviour
- experience of loss/ bereavement
- sibling relationships and sibling drug use
- other caring relationships and 'lifelines'
- secrecy, stigma and social exclusion
- impact on friendships
- level of caring for self, parents and siblings

child's developmental needs
health
education
emotional and behavioural development
identity
family and social relationships
social presentation
self-care skills

parenting capacity
basic care
ensuring safety
emotional warmth
stimulation
guidance and boundaries
stability

child
----
safeguarding and promoting welfare

family and environmental factors
family history and functioning
wider family
housing
employment
income
family's social integration
community resources

- details of drug use and impact on parental health/ behaviour/mood
- physical availability to child and impairment of ability to provide care
- emotional availability to child
- strategies to protect child from impact of drugs
- role of drugs within parental relationships/ partnership
- consistency and reliability
- priorities – drugs or child?
- messages to child about drug use and offending behaviour
- previous parenting capacity

- past drug treatment/ engagement
- offending behaviour and convictions
- who knows about drug use? And implications for wider family relationships
- extended family able to act as carers

- adequacy of material resources – money and housing
- home is exposed to risky adults or activities
- community attitudes and stigma
- support network outside the home

Activity 6
The assessment jigsaw
Aim

To enable participants to undertake holistic assessments of the needs of children affected by parental substance misuse.

> **LEARNING OBJECTIVES**
>
> By the end of the session participants will:
>
> - be more aware of the need to gather information from a wide range of sources
>
> - have been introduced to a framework to analyse that information to identify the needs of the child
>
> - have used the information gained to identify the outcomes to be achieved for the child and the services that will be needed.

Target audience

This exercise can be used with practitioners and supervisors involved in undertaking assessments of children in need.

Time

One hour.

> **TRAINING MATERIALS/AIDS**
>
> - copies of Assessment jigsaw (1): case scenario (one for each participant)
>
> - photocopies of Assessment jigsaw (2): additional information cut into individual items. There should be one set of additional information (ten pieces) on different coloured paper for each small group. These should be kept in separate envelopes for each group and colour coded
>
> - one copy of Assessment jigsaw (3): analysing the information grid per group.

Process
PART 1

1. *Introduce* the exercise by giving a brief summary or recap of the main points of the model Applying the Assessment Framework.

2. Divide participants into smaller groups of four to five participants and assign each group a colour to reflect the information you are holding.

3. Each group should spend five minutes reading the case scenario.

4. Tell the groups that the facilitators have ten additional written pieces of information about the family. Each group needs to decide what further information would be helpful for them in undertaking an assessment and, once decided, should approach the facilitators to request specifically this information for their group/colour. This should be done discreetly – to avoid being overheard by other groups. An example of this would be 'Blue team would like to find out if the family are known to Family Support. Do they have any information?' There are some agencies from whom there is no information.

5. If the trainer has this piece of information, they should give it to the group from the group's colour-coded envelope.

6. The groups should not spend too much time on evaluating the information at this stage.

7. Once each group has got its full set of information, debrief this part of the exercise. Were there any similarities between the groups over the information they struggled with? If so, why?

PART 2

8. Each group should read the information more thoroughly and then complete the grid, giving brief details of the needs, desired outcomes and services for each child.

9. The facilitator should run through the concepts to start them off:

   • needs = professional judgements about the child's developmental needs, for example health

   • outcomes = deciding which aspects of the child's needs should be addressed and describing the outcomes to be achieved, with realistic timescales

   • services = the services/intervention that should be provided to achieve the desired outcomes.

10. Reconvene into a large group and ask each group to feed back on the needs, outcomes and services for one child.

FACILITATORS' NOTES

The first part of the exercise is relatively light-hearted, and groups can compete about who will 'win'. It can also highlight narrow or stereotypical thinking (for example, a failure to talk to children or extended family, or a failure to consider the needs of the unborn child).

The second part of the exercise will help participants move from information gathering to analysis in a structured and systematic way. The identification of needs is more difficult than it sounds: people can move straight into services, for example 'This child needs a nursery', instead of thinking about the developmental need. If this model is used, participants will practise this systematic approach. The advantages of the approach are that it:

- is needs-led rather than service-led

- sets clear and measurable goals

- ensures that services are purposeful

- sets the context for reviewing whether services/intervention has been effective

- is transparent to all concerned.

RESOURCE THE ASSESSMENT JIGSAW (1): CASE SCENARIO

> **Julie – mother**
>
> **Lorna – 15**
>
> **Kirsty – two**
>
> The Assessment team has received a referral about Kirsty, aged two-and-a-half. The previous evening she had been brought to the hospital A&E department by her mother, Julie, who said that she had found her earlier that evening holding an empty bottle of methadone with no lid on it. Julie was concerned that she had drunk some, although when seen, Kirsty showed no indication of methadone ingestion. Julie refused to allow Kirsty to stay in hospital overnight for observation, but said she would return if she had any concerns.
>
> A&E staff thought Kirsty looked rather 'grubby and unkempt', but appeared happy. She seemed to have a good relationship with her mother. Julie told the hospital staff that she was pregnant.
>
> Your records show that a number of previous referrals have been dealt with by initial assessments. There have been four requests for s17 money in the last year, with Julie citing theft or problems with the Benefits Agency as the cause of her difficulties. There has also been a recent school referral about Lorna, aged 15, who was reported to have a pattern of erratic school attendance over the previous 12 months, with no attendance at all for the last academic term. In response to this, a letter was sent to Julie reminding her of her legal responsibilities for her daughter's education.

Your task

The case has been allocated to you for an initial assessment. The facilitators have a further ten pieces of important information about the family. This information comes from other professionals, and from family members.

In your groups:

1. Decide what further information you need to complete the assessment, and who you would want to speak to in order to get that information.

2. Write the agency/information requested on a piece of paper and hand it to the trainers (or ask them quietly!). They will give you any information that they have for your group.

3. Don't spend time evaluating the information at this stage, but read it to see if it gives you clues as to the additional information you might request.

RESOURCE THE ASSESSMENT JIGSAW (2): ADDITIONAL INFORMATION (page 1)

✂ ·

Extended family/grandparents

Kirsty's paternal grandparents would like to have more involvement with her. They live about two hours' distance away and can't visit very often because of poor health. They worry about Kirsty, and wish they could do more to help. Their son has another child whom he no longer sees because of allegations of domestic violence. They have already lost contact with one child, and don't want to lose contact with Kirsty as well.

✂ ·

School

Lorna was felt to be a very bright student who could have achieved well and gone on to further education. She was particularly gifted at drama and creative writing. She has not attended school at all for the last academic term, and for several months prior to that her attendance had been patchy. She is in Year 11 and due to sit her GCSE exams this summer. The school would be willing to offer intensive help to prepare for the exams. There has been no response to attempts to make contact with the family.

✂ ·

Substance misuse team

The team has known Julie for over two years. She was initially referred by her GP for a community detoxification programme using methadone. She has a six-year history of intravenous heroin use, and also uses alcohol. Julie was discharged from treatment a year ago because of non-compliance with her methadone – though she has always denied the use of heroin on top of her prescription. She was re-referred to the team by her GP about six weeks ago following the confirmation of her pregnancy. She is given a prescription of 40ml of methadone daily. Urine screens have indicated the continued use of opiates and cocaine. Julie completely denies this.

✂ ·

Police/probation

Julie's partner, who is also the father of Kirsty, has a previous conviction for selling Class A drugs with intent to supply. He served an 18-month term of imprisonment for this.

Julie was recently arrested for theft (shoplifting), and is currently on bail.

✂ ·

✂ ·

Antenatal clinic/midwife

Julie was referred to the antenatal clinic by her GP following confirmation of the pregnancy. She has failed to attend two booking appointments and a scan, and nobody at the hospital has seen her yet. At the time of the referral, six weeks ago, the GP thought she was about 18 weeks pregnant.

✂ ·

GP

You are aware that Julie has a history of intravenous heroin use and intermittent heavy alcohol use, and have referred her twice to the substance misuse team for treatment.

Both her children are registered at the health centre. You are not in a position to give any information about Lorna, who needs to give her express consent for any disclosure of her medical records. Kirsty was treated recently for an ear infection, which had been present for some time and must have been painful.

✂ ·

✂ ·

Health visitor

You have only seen Kirsty twice: once in the clinic and once at home for the 'new birth' visit. She was born prematurely, at 33 weeks. Kirsty failed to attend for two recent developmental checks, and has only had one set of immunisations. When you saw Kirsty in clinic she looked fine and was putting on weight. Julie told you that she eats well and sleeps throughout the night. The notes indicate something about a hearing test that was not followed up.

✂ ·

Mother (Julie)

You are very sorry about the incident with the methadone bottle but now think it must have been an old one that she had got hold of. You would like to move house, and don't get on with your neighbours, who think that all Glaswegians are rough, just because you speak your mind sometimes. You have split up from Kirsty's dad, but are sure that he'll be around to help once the baby is born. You would like some s17 money to get things for the baby.

✂ ·

Lorna's father

Lorna's father lives nearby and has regular contact with his daughter. He is not a drug user and is worried about Lorna being exposed to this from his ex-wife and her partner. He would like to have far more involvement with Lorna, and has been worried about how much school she has missed. His new partner, who is expecting their second child very soon, has urged him not to get involved, and he feels very torn about what to do.

✂ ·

Lorna

Lorna is desperate to leave home, though is worried about Kirsty if she did so. She looks after Kirsty most days. Lorna has an older boyfriend who is encouraging her to move in with him. If she did leave home, she would like to take Kirsty with her, as she doesn't think her mum would be able to cope.

✂ ·

RESOURCE THE ASSESSMENT JIGSAW (3): ANALYSING THE INFORMATION GRID

Thinking about the additional information you have collected, please identify the child's three most important needs, the outcomes you want to achieve for them and the services that will achieve these outcomes.

	Needs *Summarise your professional judgements about the child's needs*	**Outcomes** *Decide which aspects of the child's needs should be addressed, and describe the outcomes to be achieved. Set a realistic timescale for each outcome*	**Services** *Decide which services/ intervention will be provided to achieve the desired outcomes*
Kirsty 1. 2. 3.			
Lorna 1. 2. 3.			
Unborn baby 1. 2. 3.			

Activity 7
Specialist assessment exercise
Aim

To enable participants to consider assessments in the context of care proceedings as a result of parental drug use – and in particular the circumstances in which residential assessments would be useful.

LEARNING OBJECTIVES

By the end of the session participants will have:

- considered the nature of the evidence needed to inform decision making for children affected by parental drug use in the context of care proceedings

- gained an insight into the advantages and disadvantages of residential assessment in these circumstances.

Target audience

This exercise can be used with practitioners and supervisors involved in legal proceedings, children's guardians and solicitors or providers of specialist assessments.

Time

Forty-five minutes.

TRAINING MATERIALS/AIDS

- copy of Specialist assessment in care proceedings: a case study (page 130)

- following the exercise, copies of Practice tip 4: Considering a specialist assessment (pages 48–49) as a handout.

Process

Facilitators should remind participants of the following:

- Assessments undertaken during care proceedings will need to consider parents' ability to meet the needs of this particular child both now and in the future.

- There can sometimes be a reluctance on all sides to take such decisions when parents are battling with their own problems and there may be pressure to agree to more and more specialist assessments or to wait for the outcome of drug treatment programmes.

- The wish to assess parental capacity to change over time must be balanced against the needs of a young child for permanency.

PART 1

1. Divide participants into small groups, either in mixed or separate professional roles.

2. Give everyone a copy of the case study and ask them to spend five minutes reading it through.

3. Ask them to discuss the questions and allocate a note-taker to make brief notes of their responses.

PART 2

4. Returning to the larger group, ask each group to respond to one question before leading a general discussion.

FACILITATORS' NOTES

Facilitators may also like to be familiar with the judgement (Kent County Council vs G 2005) in which the House of Lords decided that there were restrictions in the circumstances in which a court can order local authorities to undertake assessments under s38(6) of the Children Act 1989. In future, courts can only direct such assessments if the focus of the work is on assessment of the child and their needs, and not on treatment of the parent. This is not a prohibition on residential assessments, which can still take place; it is simply a clarification of the circumstances in which the court can direct a local authority to arrange and fund them.

The sorts of issues that may be raised, or introduced by the facilitator into the discussion, are highlighted in Practice tip 4: Considering a specialist assessment.

RESOURCE SPECIALIST ASSESSMENT IN CARE PROCEEDINGS: A CASE STUDY

Miriam and Joanna (six weeks)

Miriam is a 27-year-old unmarried Kenyan woman who has lived in the UK for the last four years. She came on a student visa which has now expired. Her daughter, Joanna, is now aged six weeks and has been in hospital since birth being treated for symptoms following her mother's use of opiates (heroin) and benzodiazepines. Miriam's partner is a chaotic user of crack cocaine. He is currently in prison, but due to be released shortly. The relationship has been violent in the past.

Because of her immigration status Miriam has no income or housing entitlement. Currently homeless, she has supported herself and funded her drug use through theft and prostitution. Miriam has spoken of a period in her life, two years ago, when things went 'downhill' very suddenly. Within a short space of time she abandoned her studies and lost her savings, all her personal effects and accommodation. The local authority has concerns that she may have a history of mental health difficulties. Miriam has no family support and refuses to allow contact with her family in Kenya, as she does not wish them to know about her current circumstances.

Miriam appears devoted to Joanna. She is a frequent visitor to the hospital and provides good care. On two occasions she has visited when apparently intoxicated and smelling of alcohol. She denies any current drug use and has discharged herself from treatment. She believes that with a level of practical support – accommodation and finance – she could provide excellent care for her daughter.

Joanna is made the subject of an interim care order before she leaves hospital. The local authority plans to place her with a local foster carer with supervised contact four times a week at a family centre. Miriam would like to be given the opportunity of a residential assessment instead – one that would enable her and Joanna to be placed together. The local authority is refusing to agree to this. The nature of the assessments to be undertaken will now be the subject of a contested court hearing.

Your task

1. Can you list the pros and cons of a residential assessment in this case?

2. If the court agrees that a residential assessment must take place, what specific questions should they be asked to address?

3. If no residential assessment takes place, how else could the necessary information be made available to the court?

Activity 8
Barriers and solutions to effective practice
Aim

To enable participants to reflect on the difficulties of achieving effective practice.

NB: This could be adapted for different audiences to specify particular aspects of practice; for example, child-centred care planning, multi-agency assessment.

LEARNING OBJECTIVES

By the end of the session participants will have:

- had an opportunity to reflect on any obstacles within their current practice

- considered solutions to the obstacles identified

- helped to identify possible action that can be undertaken to achieve change.

Target audience

This exercise could be used and adapted for any audience.

Time

Forty-five minutes.

Process

1. Ask participants to divide into two equal circles, with the inner circle facing the outer.

   (a) Ask the outer circle person to speak for one minute to the person facing them on what they think are the barriers to achieving effective practice where parents use alcohol/drugs. The inner circle people must remain silent.

2. After one minute, stop the participants and move the outer circle two places to the left.

   (a) Each inner circle person takes one minute to tell the outer circle person facing them what they have just heard about the barriers.

3. Then move participants round again (so no-one sits opposite the same person twice).

   (a) Inner circle people take one minute to tell the person facing them what they think are the barriers to effective assessments/multi-agency working (one minute).

4. Move the outer circle once more, so participants are opposite a different partner. The outer circle tells their partner what they have heard so far and what they now think. Again, this should last no more than a minute.

5. Ask people to assemble into two groups – the outer circle and the inner circle.

6. On the left-hand side of flip-chart paper, each group writes down the barriers that have been identified.

7. Swap the flip-charts over. Each group chooses three barriers from the list given and identifies solutions to these – recording them on the right-hand side of the flip-chart.

8. Each group should be invited to present at least one of the barriers they selected and the solution they have devised.

9. If appropriate for the audience (for example, participants from within a single local authority) the group can identify specific actions that will be taken forward – by whom and by when.

10. It will be important that feedback and suggestions for change are noted, and that there is a consensus about what to do with the information at the conclusion of the course.

Activity 9
Thresholds for concern
Aim

To enable participants to consider the response of different agencies to children's needs and to begin the process of developing a shared understanding.

LEARNING OBJECTIVES

By the end of this session participants will have:

- explored the way in which children's needs are perceived and processed within different Assessment Frameworks

- had an opportunity to discuss any frustrations, misunderstandings or conflicts about appropriate thresholds

- considered how to improve the consistency and transparency of thresholds.

Target audience

This exercise can be used with practitioners and supervisors from a wide range of agencies – both from adult and children's services – who come into contact with adult problem alcohol and other drug users and their children.

Time

One hour.

TRAINING MATERIALS/AIDS

- copies of the Thresholds for concern exercise (page 135) for each participant.

Process

Multi-agency work is complex, and difficulties can be compounded by a lack of local policies and protocols, or even a forum for agencies to share information and talk to each other. Pressures of gatekeeping and lack of understanding of each other's roles and responsibilities mean that the focus is not always on the needs of the vulnerable child. Children's social services may be perceived as inaccessible or requiring a threshold that is deemed inappropriately high by other agencies. There may be little consensus about what circumstances present concerns about the welfare of a child.

The Common Assessment Framework aims to help practitioners in all agencies communicate and work together more effectively, as well as ensuring that assessments are undertaken in a more consistent way.

PART 1

1. Divide the large group into smaller, multi-agency groups. Try to ensure that there is a mixture of agencies represented in each of the small groups. Ask the small groups to consider the Thresholds for concern exercise and reach a consensus, if possible, about the 'right' response to each short scenario. It may not be possible to complete all the scenarios, so ask groups to start at different points.

2. Return to the larger group and ask for feedback on a selection of the scenarios. It will be most helpful to explore the situations where there was little consensus achieved within or across the groups. Ask participants to specify their reasons for the decisions taken. Discuss the similarities and differences, and why these may arise.

PART 2

3. Take general feedback of the main learning points for them all. Ask the group to share information, from the perspective of their agency, about the local implementation of the Common Assessment Framework and their familiarity with the Framework for the Assessment of Children in Need and their Families.

4. Ask them to identify two or three changes they propose to make, or have already made, as a result of the Common Assessment Framework.

FACILITATORS' NOTES

Facilitators will need to be familiar with the Framework for the Assessment of Children in Need and Their Families, the Common Assessment Framework and any local documents regarding eligibility for services or referral procedures. This should include substance misuse and children's services.

The exercise can bring out tensions between different agencies/groups of staff, and it is important to manage these without them becoming personalised or hostile. It is a useful opportunity to dispel any misconceptions between agencies about each other's roles and responsibilities.

It may also be possible, if the training takes place within local authorities, to identify a way that the dialogue can be continued.

RESOURCE THRESHOLDS FOR CONCERN EXERCISE

Which of these situations warrants a further assessment?

In your groups please rank each one:

A. no further action needed

B. consideration under the Common Assessment Framework

C. assessment by children's social services (please specify type/level of assessment if possible, e.g. s47).

1. Woman booked late (32 weeks) for antenatal care. First baby. On a methadone prescription but smoking heroin on top. Seems to have made good preparations for the baby and has good family support.	
2. Parents who smoke cannabis every night with very demanding two-year-old twins. They can't go out easily, and say it's the only way they can relax in the evenings.	
3. Three-year-old brought to A&E department with accidental methadone ingestion. The methadone was left out within reach of the child, though is normally stored securely.	
4. Baby brought to A&E department with accidental methadone ingestion. Parents had been using the calibrated feeding bottle to measure out their own methadone dose and simply had not rinsed it out afterwards.	
5. Parents stopped for a driving offence. The car was found to have drugs inside, though the children were not there at the time.	
6. Children persistently late for school and appearing unkempt and neglected. Father appears intoxicated and unsteady on his feet when he comes to collect them. He is asked about substance use, and strongly denies it.	
7. Complaints from neighbours about the disruptive behaviour of a large family on the estate. There are allegations that the parents, and older teenagers in the family, are selling drugs. The police are called regularly to the flat because of episodes of violence.	
8. Single mother of two children aged five and eight begins a relationship with a partner who has a long history of chaotic drug use. The mother of the children is not a drug user.	
9. Two-year-old child with a painful ear infection who was not taken for medical attention for ten days. The child was previously on the Child Protection Register because of concerns about neglect arising from parental alcohol and drug use. He has now been de-registered and the case closed, as circumstances are felt to have improved.	
10. Baby of four months left in the sole care of a seven-year-old brother while mother went out shoplifting to get money to buy drugs.	
11. Couple whose previous child was removed at three months because of serious neglect, a result of long-standing and chaotic drug use. Both are now drug-free and have successfully completed detoxification and rehabilitation. They are expecting their second child.	
12. Woman who is 24 weeks pregnant with her first baby. Told antenatal clinic staff that she was regularly using ecstasy and cocaine and alcohol prior to confirmation of the pregnancy. She has used no drugs or alcohol since finding out she was pregnant.	

Activity 10
Challenges for foster carers
Aim

To enable participants to reflect on difficult situations that can arise for foster carers when looking after young children whose parents are problem alcohol and other drug users, and to share helpful strategies.

> **LEARNING OBJECTIVES**
>
> By the end of the session participants will have:
>
> - had an opportunity to share their experiences and dilemmas with other carers and support staff
>
> - increased knowledge and awareness of adult problem substance use and the impact on children
>
> - heard about strategies for responding to the challenges of caring for children in these circumstances.

Target audience

This exercise can be used with foster carers, and social workers from fostering teams. It is useful for both experienced and inexperienced carers.

Time

One hour.

> **TRAINING MATERIALS/AIDS**
>
> - copies of Challenges for foster carers (pages 136–138) – enough for each participant.

Process

1. Divide participants into small groups, mixing experienced and inexperienced carers and support workers. Ask them to consider the scenarios, and suggest strategies for dealing with them.

2. Reconvene into the large group for feedback and further discussion.

> **FACILITATORS' NOTES**
>
> This exercise has been very successful in encouraging discussion about a wide range of difficulties, and participants are generally keen to offer their own experience and solutions. An approach that reinforced their expertise – for example in thinking about their contribution to care planning or challenging a medical opinion that might have been dismissive of their concerns – was particularly helpful.

RESOURCE CHALLENGES FOR FOSTER CARERS (page 1)

Your task

Here are some difficult situations that can arise when you are a foster carer looking after children whose parents are problem substance users. In your groups, can you come up with some strategies for dealing with the following situations? (Or you might decide to do nothing.)

1. You are supervising contact in your home several times a week. The social worker tells you that the parents, who were previous users of heroin, are now drug-free. You think they seem 'funny' sometimes when they come to contact – they find it hard to concentrate and leave early. You don't know much about drugs, but do wonder if they are using alcohol. You can't really put your finger on what's wrong, so you don't feel happy about saying anything. They're doing very well and you don't want to cause trouble.

2. You have taken a baby straight from hospital after being treated for withdrawal symptoms. The paediatrician says the baby is fine now and doesn't need to come back. You find the baby very difficult to manage – difficult to pacify and feed – and she wants to be carried all the time. She seems very uncomfortable and rarely sleeps for long. The GP and health visitor say there is nothing wrong.

3. You have just started looking after the fifth baby born to a very chaotic drug-using mother. All the other children have been adopted. You feel very strongly that drug use is wrong and that women who use drugs should not be allowed to have children. The social worker, whom you think is very young and naïve, is talking about rehabilitation and wants you to take the baby to contact.

RESOURCE CHALLENGES FOR FOSTER CARERS
(page 2)

4. You have become very friendly with a young mother who has contact once a week. Both she and her partner have had a hard life and were 'in care' themselves. Father's attendance at contact is erratic, and sometimes you wonder if there is domestic violence. Mother is keen that you give good feedback about them both to the social worker. You feel in a difficult position, and want to be supportive, but have a nagging worry about the father. Should you say anything?

5. You think some money was missing from your purse after a recent contact visit. You feel awkward about saying anything in case the parents think you're picking on them just because they're drug users.

Activity 11
Contact issues
Aim

To enable participants to reflect on the potentially difficult situations that can arise for foster carers around contact, and to share experiences and strategies with other foster carers.

LEARNING OBJECTIVES

By the end of the session participants will have:

- increased awareness of the particular benefits and challenges arising from contact with birth families for children affected by parental problem alcohol and other drug use

- increased confidence in sharing their difficulties with other carers and support staff

- strategies and suggestions for dealing with problems about contact.

Target audience

This exercise can be used with foster carers and social workers from fostering teams. It is useful for both experienced and inexperienced carers.

Time

Forty-five minutes. This could be longer if participants wish to discuss their own experiences.

TRAINING MATERIALS/AIDS

- flip-chart paper and pens

- scenario below, written on flip-chart paper or PowerPoint slide

- copies of Practice tip 3: Thinking about care planning (page 47) as a handout.

Process
PART 1

1. As a large group, ask participants to identify the challenges and benefits of contact for such children in both short-term and long-term placements. These could be written up on a flip-chart. They could include assessment of rehabilitation, to reassure them that parents are all right, to build up a realistic picture of their parents' problems.

PART 2

2. Ask the group to imagine the scenario:

    > You are caring for a new baby placed on an interim care order straight from hospital. The baby has been treated for withdrawal symptoms. She is no longer on medication but is still quite an irritable and difficult baby to look after. This is a first baby for both parents, who are drug users who are also known to have used alcohol to excess. The parents have recently had treatment for their drug use, but the alcohol use seems to have been sidelined. Contact is part of the assessment about whether or not the baby can return home. It has been arranged four times a week – twice in your home and twice in a family centre.

3. Divide participants into two groups and ask the foster carers to consider what sort of issues and problems are likely to arise for them about these contact arrangements. (These could be things like unreliability of the parents, safety in the home, parental criticism of the care given, disagreement with the care plan, insufficient background information.)

4. Ask the groups then to pick out the three issues they consider most significant and note them down on flip-chart paper.

5. Ask the group to swap notes and come up with solutions or advice to the foster carer in these circumstances; for example, if parents are unreliable in keeping to the identified times, a solution could be a written contract with the social worker.

6. Go through the responses as a larger group.

FACILITATORS' NOTES

The first part of the exercise ensures that the needs of the child are at the centre of the task. Children with parents who use drugs and alcohol problematically face many challenges in dealing with the consequences of parental alcohol/drug use. They may have difficulty relinquishing adult roles and worry about what will happen to their parents.

Carers are likely to be keen to share their own difficulties and experiences. Feedback from workshops where this discussion took place indicated that it was highly valued by the workshop participants, with the advice of more experienced carers being found particularly useful.

Activity 12
Reflecting on practice
Aim

An opportunity for managers to reflect on local practice in working with families where children are affected by problem alcohol and other drug use.

LEARNING OBJECTIVES

By the end of the session participants will have:

- gained insight into local practice – how their social work service is responding to referrals and conducting assessments

- reflected on the strengths and weaknesses of the response

- considered barriers to effective practice and any changes needed.

Target audience

Managers and social work supervisors in children's social services, child protection managers and conference chairs, independent reviewing officers.

Time

One hour.

TRAINING MATERIALS/AIDS

- copies of Reflecting on practice case examples and grid, or a sample of local cases, could be prepared. These would need to be drawn from a variety of teams, with identifying information removed to avoid individuals feeling criticised

- copies of Recent research and policy (pages 30–36) or Practice tips (pages 44–51).

Process

1. Divide participants into small groups, mixed across teams and areas of responsibility.

2. Give each participant the pre-prepared case examples and each group the grid for recording their response.

3. Ask each group to identify and record:

   - What do you think is going on for this child? What are their possible unmet needs?

   - What level of assessment, if any, would be needed to assess this need?

4. Reconvening as a large group, ask each group in turn to feed back their responses to a case and allow discussion.

5. If local scenarios have been used, tell participants about what actually happened in each case, for example case closed without a visit.

6. Facilitate a large group discussion:

   • Is there a consensus about what constitutes good practice?

   • If there was a difference between the ideal response and actual practice, why did this happen?

   • What are the barriers to effective practice?

   • Is there any action that needs to be taken?

FACILITATORS' NOTES

This exercise was undertaken in the two pilot authorities using actual anonymised case material from the social work files. It proved very useful in stimulating discussion about current practice, and the value was greatly enhanced by the use of actual case material. It was important to select cases that had gone well in addition to cases where, in hindsight, practice could and should have been undertaken differently. Participants were honest and reflective about their practice.

RESOURCE REFLECTING ON PRACTICE

Case examples

1. A 15-year-old girl (A) has been referred by her mother, expressing concerns that A is beyond her control – shoplifting, truanting and smoking cannabis. The file indicated unsubstantiated concerns about sexual abuse several years ago. The father of A has been recently imprisoned for drug-related offences. The mother of A has a history of drug use but says she is now abstinent. A member of the extended family has offered to care for A to give her mother respite, but cannot do so without financial support from the local authority.

2. Referral for a pre-birth assessment made by a midwife at the antenatal clinic. A woman has recently booked for antenatal care; she is 33 weeks pregnant with her first baby. The woman has disclosed a long history of chaotic drug use, including intravenous opiates and cocaine. Her partner is in prison for drug-related offences. The woman is homeless and has frequent changes of accommodation.

3. A referral from a probation officer supervising a father on a DTTO. Father is a single parent with two children aged three and six years. He admits to drinking to 'help him get through'. He has recently begun to test positive for opiates and is becoming unreliable about keeping appointments, saying child care commitments render this difficult. Probation had referred the case six weeks ago when he had left the children unattended at home whilst he attended an office appointment with them. On this occasion children's social services had not instigated any assessment but had written to the father expressing concern about the incident.

4. Referral for a pre-birth assessment made by a community midwife. The referral concerns a young woman who is 26 weeks pregnant with her first child. Both she and her partner have a long history of drug use and offending, and the relationship is violent. Father has mental health difficulties. Both parents are in receipt of treatment for their drug use but continue to use heroin on top of their methadone prescription. There is very good support from both sides of the extended family.

5. Referral from an estate manager about a single parent with three children aged 15, 13 and two. Neighbours have been reporting concerns about the house being used for drug dealing, alleging that the mother and her eldest daughter are selling and using drugs from the property, and there are frequent fights and disturbances there. The case has been the subject of several initial assessments following similar previous referrals from housing and the police.

6. A seven-day-old baby has been referred by staff on the hospital neonatal unit. The baby has been showing signs of opiate withdrawal syndrome, and the mother says that she is a 'recreational' user of heroin – this had not been known about in the pregnancy. Records indicate a previous referral to social services in identical circumstances two years earlier following the birth of her first child at a different hospital. Mother is aged 30. Her partner works full time and both parents have supportive family who live locally.

RESOURCE REFLECTING ON PRACTICE GRID

Case number	What are the possible unmet needs of this child?	What level of assessment, if any, would you need to undertake, e.g. NFA, initial assessment, core assessment, s47 enquiries? What other enquiries and actions are indicated?
1		
2		
3		
4		
5		
6		

Activity 13
Presentation on alcohol and drug use in pregnancy
Aim

To describe the physical effects that maternal alcohol/drug use may have on unborn and newborn children.

LEARNING OBJECTIVES

By the end of the session participants will have:

- heard about the effects that different drugs may have on unborn children

- gained some understanding of withdrawal symptoms and treatment

- considered the implications for babies' subsequent care.

Target audience

This exercise can be used with practitioners or foster carers involved with unborn or young babies.

Time

Thirty minutes.

TRAINING MATERIALS/AIDS

- PowerPoint presentation, available to download from the JKP website.

Process

- Presentation by the facilitator using the following slides.

- Short group discussion.

Options

Alternative presentations could be developed based on other materials in the toolkit from the Key messages section.

Drug use in pregnancy

- Can affect unborn babies directly or indirectly because of mother's health problems

- Poly-drug use common and effects difficult to predict

- Women may neglect own health – poor diet, smoking and alcohol use, risk of STIs, IV risks

- Lack of antenatal care and late booking

Opiates (heroin or methadone)

- Unborn baby will become dependent if used regularly

- Unborn baby will suffer withdrawal symptoms if mother does – can lead to obstetric complications

- Methadone prescribed for pregnant women to reduce this risk – has longer lasting effects than heroin

- If unborn baby becomes dependent, will have withdrawal symptoms after birth

- Babies at increased risk of low birth weight and poor growth. May have smaller head size and born pre-term

Cocaine and amphetamines

- Stimulants affect appetite and lead to poor diet

- No substitute drug prescribed

- Increased risk of low birth weight and prematurity. Cocaine is associated with range of serious obstetric complications

- No predictable pattern of withdrawal – muscular twitching and irritability common

- Emerging concerns about developmental delay and poor concentration by school-age children

Cannabis

- Most common drug used in pregnancy

- Consequences similar to use of nicotine

- Regular use associated with low birth weight and prematurity

'Prescription' drugs

- Benzodiazepines (e.g. diazepam and temazepam) commonly used as part of repertoire of drug use

- Increased risk of low birth weight and prematurity

- Can cause serious withdrawal symptoms in newborn babies – similar to opiate withdrawal

- Effects of withdrawal can last for several months – 'floppy baby syndrome'

Withdrawal symptoms

- Antenatal exposure to opiates and benzodiazepines may cause withdrawal

- Severity and duration difficult to predict

- Symptoms emerge 24–72 hours after birth

- Symptoms can include shaking or jerky movements, high-pitched crying, feeding difficulties, sneezing, sensibility to light or stimulus, vomiting and diarrhoea

- Severity of symptoms not necessarily related to level of antenatal exposure

Treatment for withdrawal

- Can be on special care baby units or on postnatal wards

- Sedative drugs used – can include morphine and anti-convulsants

- Aim is to reduce distress and allow sleeping and feeding while baby 'grows out' of withdrawal

- Careful handling techniques – swaddling, massage and 'kangaroo care' can be helpful

- Timescales very difficult to predict

Implications

- Pregnancy is the best time for professionals to get involved

- Parents' behaviour during pregnancy indicates future parenting ability

- There may be unrealistic expectations about becoming drug-free

- The neonatal period can be very stressful for parents, e.g. guilt, separation if baby on SCBU, family's criticism, irritable/sleepy baby, multiple appointments, case conferences

Foetal alcohol syndrome/foetal alcohol spectrum disorder

- Dilemmas of consumption and definition – most often an invisible birth defect

- New research interests

- Advice to pregnant women and pre-conception

Foetal alcohol syndrome/spectrum disorder

- Physical; psychological; behavioural; neurological difficulties

- FAS – heavy maternal alcohol use

- 4–5% children born to women who consumed large amounts of alcohol during pregnancy – affected by full syndrome presentation

- Pattern and duration of drinking are important considerations in defining risk (BMA 2007)

Alcohol in pregnancy

- WHO (World Health Organization) – abstinence – no known safe levels

- Other research

- RCM (2010) recommends that midwives advise pregnant women about the risks of consuming alcohol and to avoid alcohol while pregnant and breastfeeding

Damage caused by alcohol in the developing foetus is dependent on:

- Level of maternal alcohol consumption

- Pattern of alcohol exposure

- Stage of pregnancy when alcohol is consumed

Risk factors:

- Genetic make-up of mother and foetus

- Nutritional state of mother

- Hormonal interaction

- Poly-drug use (including tobacco)

- General health of mother

- Stress

- Low socioeconomic status

How much, when

- All trimesters have been associated with abnormalities and no upper limit of alcohol is known

- Stage determines how and which cells of developing foetus are affected

- Critical periods of exposure occur during first and third trimester

Activity 14
Supervision
Aim

To identify the obstacles to effective supervision and to enable managers to reflect on key messages for practice where children are affected by parental problem alcohol and other drug use.

LEARNING OBJECTIVES

By the end of the session participants will have:

- reflected on their 'quality control' role in relation to work undertaken with such children

- had the opportunity to apply their supervision skills to such cases.

Target audience

Managers and social work supervisors in children's social services.

This exercise could be most usefully undertaken after the previous exercise looking at local practice.

Time

Thirty minutes.

TRAINING MATERIALS/AIDS

- copies of the Supervision scenario (page 155)

- handouts of Practice tip 1 (pages 44–45) and Practice tip 2 (page 46) for distribution at the end of the exercise.

Process

1. Ask participants to form pairs and nominate one person as a supervisor and one person as a supervisee in order to role play, for five minutes, a supervision session based on the scenario given. Supervisees can improvise and bring in past experiences.

2. After five minutes, divide participants into two groups – one of supervisors and one of supervisees.

3. Ask each group to:

   - identify what, if anything, was getting in the way of effective decision making for this child

   - draw up a list of common difficulties and pitfalls when supervising such cases

   - identify what helped to unlock the process.

4. Return to the larger group for feedback from the exercise.

FACILITATORS' NOTES

The following are prompts to aid discussion if participants do not identify them:

- over-optimism

- disguised compliance

- exclusion of fathers

- focus on parental problems at the expense of the child

- failure to elicit information from other agencies or the extended family

- lack of knowledge about adult problem substance use and/or its implications for parenting.

The group may come up with others, for example unwillingness to be seen as judgemental or stigmatising, lack of clarity about confidentiality, difficulties in dealing with denial or minimisation and resistant families.

RESOURCE SUPERVISION SCENARIO

J is a 22-year-old woman who has been referred to the advice and assessment team by staff at the community substance misuse team. She is 30 weeks pregnant and booked at the local hospital for the birth of her first child. J has been in receipt of a methadone prescription for more than 18 months and she regularly uses alcohol. During her pregnancy she has been regularly using heroin and temazepam on top of her methadone. She still attends for planned appointments with her key worker, but is felt to be generally less engaged than previously. If such use continues, she will be discharged from treatment once the baby is born.

J's partner is not personally known to the treatment services. He is said to be a heroin user who has been imprisoned for drug-related offences. Other service users describe him as being a dealer.

A home visit for an initial assessment was carried out. J was polite and cooperative and understood the concerns of children's social services. She said she was attending regularly for antenatal care and gave absolute assurances that she would not use unprescribed drugs in the future, now she was aware of the possible impact on the baby. J said that she and her partner were no longer together, although he and his family will have some level of contact with the baby. This is also his first child.

The home conditions were very good, and J, who had previously worked as a teacher, had made a great deal of preparation for the baby. J also said she had very good support from her own mother and sister, who lived nearby.

The social worker's view is that there are no grounds for concern and they are recommending that the case be closed. The drugs team or the hospital would be asked to re-refer in the future if appropriate to do so.

Your task
Role-play, for five minutes, a supervision session based on the above scenario.

4

Briefings

In the course of the project, practitioners highlighted the topics that they would like to know more about in order to support their practice. This section attempts to provide useful information with this in mind.

Caring for the pregnant drug user

This is an edited version of 'Caring for the Pregnant Drug User' by Mary Hepburn, consultant obstetrician at Princess Royal Maternity Hospital, Glasgow. The chapter originally appeared in Care of Drug Users in General Practice *(Beaumont 2004).*

Drug-using women, like all women, need appropriate reproductive health care to protect and control their fertility and to ensure they have healthy pregnancies if and when they choose (Advisory Council on the Misuse of Drugs 2003; Scottish Executive 2003). Reproductive health care for drug-using women should be provided by multidisciplinary teams within services that are easily accessible by any route, including self-referral. The different components of reproductive health care should be provided as a continuum either by a single service or by services working in close collaboration to make sure that women do not fall into the gaps that often exist between mainstream services. Primary care offers such continuity, and is therefore ideally placed to provide or coordinate much of this care.

Fertility and general reproductive health

Heroin (and any other drug that causes a chaotic lifestyle with poor diet and weight loss) can reduce fertility and can cause amenorrhoea – the absence or suppression of periods. However, the two effects are not always linked, so that women can be amenorrhoeic but fertile. Any treatment like methadone that stabilises lifestyle and improves general health will increase fertility, and this can occur before menstruation resumes. All women attending for drug treatment should be advised about this, and if they do not want to become pregnant, given effective contraception.

To protect both their fertility and any pregnancy they may have, women should be screened for sexually transmitted infections and given information about blood-borne virus infections, with an offer of screening. They should be given information about the effects of drugs, smoking and alcohol on pregnancy. When they want to conceive it is important that they have a settled lifestyle, with their drug use, smoking and alcohol consumption stabilised at the lowest achievable level.

Effects of drugs on pregnancy

Drug use is associated with higher rates of mortality and morbidity (incidence of disease) for mother and baby. However, the drugs commonly used have limited direct effects on pregnancy, with most of the adverse effects being due to poor general health and chaotic lifestyle, together with other health and social factors common among women from disadvantaged backgrounds.

Long-acting methadone does not carry the increased risk of pre-term labour associated with the use of short-acting heroin, and there is also considerable evidence of methadone's other medical and short-term benefits. Available information on the effects of buprenorphine (this is also known as Subutex) suggests that, dose for dose, it is similar to methadone. While methadone remains the opiate substitute of choice, women stabilised on buprenorphine at the time of conception can be maintained on this during the pregnancy. All opiates can cause withdrawal symptoms in the baby. Those due to dihydrocodeine (also known as DF118) can be especially severe, but otherwise there seems to be little difference in severity – although withdrawal due to methadone is later in onset and more prolonged.

Benzodiazepines increase the risk of cleft palate, but the risk to the individual foetus is still small. They also cause neonatal withdrawals that are especially severe, often prolonged, and are less easily treated than those due to opiates. Withdrawals due to combined opiate and benzodiazepine use are disproportionately severe and difficult to treat. No other drug use causes significant neonatal withdrawal, although alcohol and tobacco can cause mild withdrawals that do not need treatment.

Cocaine use can cause placental separation and pre-term rupture of the membranes, with many other effects variously reported. However, adverse effects seem largely confined to heavy chaotic use of cocaine, especially crack cocaine. Alcohol causes reduced foetal growth and, rarely in the UK, the combination of effects known as foetal alcohol syndrome.

Foetal alcohol syndrome/foetal alcohol spectrum disorder (FASD)

Drinking during pregnancy can cause brain damage, leading to a range of developmental, cognitive and behavioural problems which can appear at any time during childhood.

The effects of exposure to alcohol at any point during pregnancy creates a risk of life-long damage to the brain and the nervous system of the unborn child. FASD is the umbrella term for different diagnoses which include:

- foetal alcohol syndrome

- partial foetal alcohol syndrome

- alcohol-related neuro-development disorder

- alcohol-related birth defects.

Many factors can complicate the identification of FASD, but decades of laboratory research and animal studies have proved that alcohol alone can cause significant problems (Children in Scotland 2011). Children affected by FASD can display a variety of learning difficulties and behaviour problems. These are primarily the result of impairment of the brain's ability to plan, learn from experiences and control impulses. There can be some physical damage associated with foetal alcohol syndrome, including facial characteristics. However, these are usually caused by very heavy drinking during the pregnancy and are not obvious to non-experts. Most often FASD is an invisible birth defect (Children in Scotland 2011).

There is growing evidence from across the world to back up the hypothesis that foetal alcohol harm causes serious human, social and economic costs (Carpenter *et al.* 2014; Riley 2011).

Further information and support can be obtained from the National Organisation for Foetal Alcohol Syndrome – UK (www.nofas-uk.org), which is dedicated to support for people affected by FASD and their families and communities.

Management of pregnant drug-using women

Care should be provided by a multidisciplinary team. Early stabilisation of drug use is important. Detoxification from opiates is safe at any speed and at any stage of pregnancy but should only be undertaken if appropriate. Detoxification from benzodiazepines is safe for the foetus, but cover with a short reducing dose of diazepam is advisable to prevent maternal convulsions. Women using methadone as well as benzodiazepines should reduce and if possible discontinue the latter first, and the dose of methadone may need to be increased to help them do so. There is no evidence to support maintenance therapy for any other type of drug apart from opiates. Whilst stabilisation at the lowest comfortable dose is the objective, external factors may influence stability and the dose may need to be varied (up or down) throughout the pregnancy. Pregnant drug-using women should be offered screening for HIV, hepatitis B and hepatitis C.

A detailed scan at 18–20 weeks is justified for women using benzodiazepines, but maternity care should otherwise be according to individual circumstances. Additional monitoring for the foetus is only needed if there are clinical concerns, but it is important to remember that these women have potentially high-risk pregnancies. They are therefore not suitable for midwife-only care, although much of their care can be delivered by midwives. General medical and social problems should be addressed. A multidisciplinary meeting at 32 weeks gestation allows identification of problems, setting of goals and planning of management.

The vulnerable babies of drug-using women will especially benefit from breast feeding, which will also reduce the severity of the neonatal drug withdrawals. All drug-using women (except those who are HIV positive) should be encouraged to breast feed regardless of drugs used, dose or pattern of use. Breast feeding is not contraindicated for women who are hepatitis C positive.

Social support should include support with parenting and be continued after postnatal discharge. However, there should be a clear distinction between family support and child protection, with the latter separately addressed only if necessary.

Key points

- Women who use alcohol and drugs problematically need comprehensive reproductive health care provided as a continuum to protect and control their fertility.

- If provided with appropriate services, drug/alcohol-using women attending regularly for care can have healthy pregnancies at times of their choosing.

Black and minority ethnic drug use

This briefing originally appeared in Care of Drug Users in General Practice *(Beaumont 2004), and is reproduced with the permission of the author, Dima Abdulrahim.*

Prevalence and patterns of drug use

Prevalence rates of drug use among black and minority ethnic (BME) populations are lower than those of the majority white population; low levels are particularly evident among South Asians and black Africans. Although overall levels of drug use are similar among black Caribbeans and whites, this is largely because of the high use of cannabis in the former group (Ramsey *et al.* 2001).

However, drug use among BME populations is significant and is increasing. Moreover, a combination of factors that characterise the lives of many BME people, in particular risk factors that revolve around social exclusion and deprivation, means that the context within which drug use exists provides an environment in which it can be particularly problematic (Fountain *et al.* 2003).

Studies suggest that, overall, BME populations use a similar range of substances to their white peers. There are, however, different patterns and different levels of problematic drug use among the different groups. African Caribbeans are more likely than all other groups to present to services for a primary crack cocaine problem, and problematic use may also focus on cannabis. This does not mean that these communities are not affected by heroin; individuals do present to services for opiate users and, whilst smoking is more common, injecting does occur. Heroin use often starts in prison or is started to manage the comedown from crack.

Heroin is often the drug of choice of South Asian populations, who are more likely to smoke than inject. However, there is some evidence of injecting and anecdotal evidence of an increase in injecting, especially amongst young people. The low uptake of needle exchange facilities is a cause for concern, as is possible lack of knowledge about transmission of blood-borne infections (Sangster *et al.* 2002). Little is known about drug use among newly arriving communities, including refugees and asylum seekers. The use of khat is restricted to Somalis, and some problematic use has been noted. Heroin use has been noted amongst Vietnamese and Turkish-speaking communities.

Uptake of treatment

There is strong evidence that BME drug users – and South Asians in particular – are under-represented in treatment services throughout the country. This may not be so much the case in London, but even in the capital, whilst African Caribbean and Indian drug users are utilising drug services, black Africans, Pakistanis and Bangladeshis are under-represented, as are drug users from more recently established communities. There is also plenty of anecdotal evidence that services are not able to retain BME users in treatment. However, where there is concerted effort to work with these groups, good retention rates can be achieved (Harocopos *et al.* 2003).

Evidence about how BME patients perceive the accessibility of drug treatment within primary care is contradictory. Some studies show that South Asian and other BME drug users would be more likely to approach a GP than a drug service, and commentators have recommended the development of such services (Chaudry, Sherlock and Patel 1997; Johnson and Carroll 1995). Another study showed that, on the contrary, BME users – and South Asians in particular – were less likely to see their GP about their drug use than their white peers, and in some instances the differences were striking (Sangster *et al.* 2002).

Barriers to uptake of treatment

Studies have identified a number of barriers to the uptake of drug treatment in all settings:

- denial that drug use exists in some communities (e.g. South Asian), by communities and professionals alike

- fear of breach of confidentiality

- ethnicity of staff

- lack of understanding of BME cultures (Sangster *et al.* 2002)

- lack of appropriate service response in terms of:

  - under-development of treatment for crack cocaine (Harocopos *et al.* 2003)

  - paucity of response to cannabis

  - opiate focus of drug treatment, especially by community services

  - harm reduction focus on injecting; needs of non-injectors often marginalised

  - residential rehabilitation services analysed as least capable of meeting the needs of diverse populations (Sangster *et al.* 2002).

Key points

- Drug use prevalence rates among BME populations are lower than in the general population, but are nonetheless significant, increasing and exist in a high-risk context of social exclusion.

- Issues to be considered include cannabis use, a response to crack use and poor knowledge of transmission of blood-borne infections.

- GPs are in a unique position to work with BME users as they often have substantial experience of dealing with the needs of culturally and socially diverse populations.

Understanding drugs

This briefing provides basic information about 'problem' drug use, the range of drugs that may be misused and treatment options.

Definitions

Drug use is common in the UK, and many people will describe themselves as recreational drug users. This suggests that their use is under control and does not require intervention. Terms such as abuse/misuse/addiction are used to describe 'heavier end' drug use, but are often used interchangeably without agreed definitions. They depend more on the values of the person using them than the behaviour itself. A more useful descriptor is *dependence*, which is a compulsion to continue taking a drug. If this is to avoid the physical discomfort of withdrawal, it is a physical dependence (or addiction). Withdrawal is the body's reaction to the sudden absence of a drug on which it has become physically dependent. If the compulsion has a psychological basis – the need for stimulation or pleasure or the need for a chemical 'crutch' – then it's referred to as psychological dependence. Psychological dependence is the most difficult to overcome.

The most useful way of understanding the issue is to think in terms of 'problem drug users'. This helps to identify the point at which the use of drugs becomes harmful:

S/he experiences social, psychological, physical or legal problems related to intoxication and/or excessive consumption and/or dependence as a consequence of her/his own use of drugs and other chemical substances.

This concentrates on the consequences of the drug use and the pattern of use rather than the drug itself. A stable (and wealthy) heroin user may not fit the definition, whilst someone else taking prescribed Valium does. This is particularly useful when considering the possible impact on parenting.

Social problems may include poverty, stigmatisation or rejection by family and friends. Psychological problems may be a direct effect of the drug itself, such as paranoia, but may also be caused by the psychological dependence that can result. Physical dangers can include the risk of overdose, health problems arising from injecting or self-neglect, and accidents. Legal problems may be caused by the illegal nature of the drugs used, but can also arise from criminal activity to fund the drug use.

Alcohol should be described as a drug because that is what it is. However, focusing on alcohol is a greater challenge than we perhaps recognise. Its legality, easy availability, its allure as a lifestyle product and its symbolic status affect our attitudes, beliefs and practices. Our society, and particularly our children, are at risk of alcohol-related harm and therefore problems associated with alcohol consumption should be understood.

Alcohol dependence is a previous psychiatric diagnosis which can be described as physically and psychologically dependent on drinking alcohol. In 2013 it was reclassified as alcohol use disorder along with alcohol abuse in *DSM-5* (Alcohol Misuse – NHS Choices 2015).

Drugs and their effects

The following refers to illegal drugs and the misuse of prescription drugs. Current street prices may be useful as an aid to assessment (see www.drugscope.org.uk), although there will be regional variations and prices are not static. Most problem drug users use drugs in combination, and alcohol is often part of the repertoire. Drugs may have a stimulant, depressive or hallucinogenic effect. Two stimulants or two depressants taken together will produce an enhanced effect. Mixing different sorts of drugs is likely to have more unpredictable consequences.

Drug	Slang names	How is it used?	Effects on the user	Withdrawal symptoms	Possible implications for parenting
Heroin	Gear, brown, junk, smack	Can be smoked ('chasing the dragon'), snorted or injected; physically addictive	Drowsiness, poor cough reflex, itchiness; pin-prick pupils; sense of warmth, wellbeing and detachment	Flu-like symptoms, dilated pupils, aching limbs, restlessness, sweating, anxiety	Social, legal and financial difficulties – neglect of self and others; physical and emotional unavailability; drowsiness; children may not be a priority over drugs
Cocaine	Charlie, white, coke	Snorted or injected	Reduced appetite, indifference to pain or fatigue; dilated pupils; garrulous; feeling alert and confident	Anxiety, irritability and restlessness, nausea	Disinhibition; acute irritability and restlessness; repeated users can appear nervous, excitable and paranoid
Crack cocaine	Rocks, wash, chips, stones	Smoked in a pipe	As above, but effects are more intense, happen more quickly and are of shorter duration	Not physically addictive but very rapid compulsion to repeat the experience	Effects as for cocaine; users have a tendency to binge and use large amounts within a short space of time
Amphetamine sulphate	Speed, billy, whizz	Snorted, smoked, swallowed or injected; can be in the form of powder or tablets	Reduced appetite; increase in confidence and energy; constant chewing motion	Extreme fatigue and hunger ('borrowed energy'); tension, anxiety, depression, irritability	Irritability and restlessness; tiredness and difficulty in concentrating after effects have worn off
Methamphetamine	Crystal meth, meth, ice, tina	Snorted, injected; smoked (as ice)	Euphoria and exhilaration; disinhibition	Rise in body temperature and blood pressure; not physically addictive but users develop strong psychological dependence	Overuse can evoke paranoia, memory loss, pronounced mood swings and unpredictable and aggressive behaviour
Benzodiazepines (tranquillisers)	Temazepam, Rohypnol, Ativan, Mogadon, Librium, Valium	Tablet form of various strengths: 2mg, 5mg and 10mg	Users feel relaxed, calm and disinhibited	Withdrawal must be done under medical supervision; can lead to panic attacks and seizures; physically addictive	Drowsiness and forgetfulness; very dangerous if taken with alcohol

Drug	Slang names	How is it used?	Effects on the user	Withdrawal symptoms	Possible implications for parenting
Ecstasy	E, doves, hug drug	Tablets of varying appearances	Hallucinogenic stimulant; increase in energy and euphoria	Tiredness and depression; risk of overheating and dehydration	(Inappropriate?) feelings of warmth towards others; disinhibition
Cannabis	Weed, blow, puff, draw, ganja, skunk, wacky backy	Dark brown resinous lump, or leaves, stalks and seeds (skunk is a hybrid cannabis which is very strong)	Relaxation and feeling of mellowness; users can become talkative; use can bring on a craving for food (the 'munchies')	Tiredness and lack of energy	There are conflicting views on the links between cannabis use and mental health difficulties; not physically addictive but users can become dependent
Alcohol	Booze	Bottles, cans	Disinhibited behaviour, risk taking. Greater propensity to violent reaction	Withdrawal, shaking, nausea, hangover. Severe problem drinking requires professional support and medical supervision	Lack of physical and emotional support. Disinhibited behaviour. Loss of control

Alcohol/drug treatment

Treatment has major benefits for alcohol and other drug users and their families; some adult alcohol/drug users can become substance-free with no outside help or substitute prescription, but many need the additional help and support offered by a treatment programme. Abstinence is a long-term goal: most alcohol and other drug users will go through many cycles of treatment, abstinence and relapse before achieving this. Nevertheless there is a growing body of research into recovery which should be known and recognised (Whitee 2011).

Detoxification

This is the physical elimination of a drug from the body. It can be achieved either by stopping the drug abruptly ('cold turkey') or the prescription of a substitute drug in gradually reducing doses. Treatment is usually offered while people are living in the community over several months, but there are a small number of in-patient units or residential detoxification units for people in particular crisis. The aim is to become drug-free, but detoxification alone does not tackle the complex issues as to why people take drugs. The relapse rate may be high if the social and psychological aspects are not also treated.

Substitute drugs used may be:

- **Methadone.** This is the usual drug of choice for treating heroin addiction. It is a synthetic opioid, physically addictive like heroin, but contains no dangerous impurities. It is a substitute for heroin and will simply prevent the development of withdrawal symptoms. Because of slow clearance from the body, the treatment is seen as safe in pregnancy. Like any opioid, it is dangerous in overdose – and particularly dangerous if used by children. It is prescribed in the form of linctus. There is a significant evidence base for the effectiveness and safety of methadone when used appropriately.

- **Subutex** (also known as buprenorphine). This works primarily by blocking the effect of heroin on the receptors of the brain. It is usually taken as a tablet dissolved under the tongue, and because of this, supervised consumption takes longer. Subutex is safer than methadone in overdose and also relatively safer for children if accidentally consumed.

- **Medication for withdrawal.** There is no direct substitute for many other problem drugs, so withdrawal symptoms may be treated by sedatives such as diazepam plus medication to control diarrhoea and spasms, which may arise.

Harm minimisation

An approach to drug use aims, not to make people become drug-free if this is an unrealistic goal for them, but to reduce the harmful effects of their continuing drug use. This may be in terms of criminal activity, social exclusion or health. The approach is characterised by community-based support services, needle exchanges and programmes that allow for methadone maintenance rather than reduction. There have also been some experiments in prescribing heroin rather than a substitute for some users.

Alcohol

Symptoms of withdrawal may be alleviated by the prescription of benzodiazepines. Harm reduction in the alcohol field has a controversial history, and abstinence is usually advocated by those who have experienced alcohol problems in the past. Naltrexone and acamprosate may be used to reduce cravings. Disulfiram will be prescribed as an incentive not to drink as it causes stomach problems if alcohol continues to be used.

Supportive services

Pharmacological treatments are highly effective, but it is important to recognise that treatment is not just about prescribing substitute medication or the relief of symptoms. Alongside medication, effective treatment will require a wide range of other interventions; for example, there is increasing interest in the use of motivational interviewing as a useful technique. There is a long established tradition of alcohol counselling in the UK (Alcohol Concern). Alcoholics Anonymous and its attendant groups such as Al-anon and Al-ateen are also well established supports.

Counselling and support with social issues such as housing, benefits, debt management and child care are also very important, as are the learning of new skills or choice of different activities to fill the day. Some supportive services involve people who have experienced drug problems at first hand, either by employing ex-users or through self-help organisations such as Narcotics Anonymous.

Rehabilitation

Rehabilitation is designed not to deal with people's physical dependence on alcohol and other drugs but to help them to establish a different way of life which does not have alcohol/drugs at the centre, so that they are able to remain alcohol/drug-free. It aims to tackle the social and psychological dependence on alcohol/drugs, and most rehabilitation projects expect users to be 'clean' or stabilised on a low dose of methadone (for drug users) before entry. Projects may be run as residential or community-based programmes, and adopt a range of approaches. Community-based services can be provided by a structured day programme, day centres, drop-ins and support groups. Residential units vary considerably in how they operate, and include a number of therapeutic communities. Funding is usually accessed through the local treatment services or community substance misuse team.

There are very few residential rehabilitation units that will also accept children, and again these vary in the support they offer: some offer a level of assessment of family functioning, whilst others focus on the needs of the adult and would not claim expertise in children's development. It will be important to establish this when deciding whether an application is appropriate. Funding can be problematic because of the need to negotiate between adult and children's services. Is this placement needed to support the adult or to enable the child to have a family life? A ruling (Kent County Council vs G. and others 2005) confirmed that children's services could not be ordered to pay for such a placement within care proceedings if the main aim was to treat the parent.

How is treatment provided?

There are various routes into drug treatment in the UK. Users enter these programmes either voluntarily or, increasingly, via the criminal justice system. There may be waiting lists for certain types of treatment, particularly those based on substitute prescribing.

PRIMARY CARE

GP-led substance misuse services are often known as shared care or primary care based treatment. The most common treatment programme is where an alcohol or drug user is managed by a GP in partnership with colleagues from adult-based treatment services. This could be a substance misuse worker, an addiction nurse or other colleagues, depending on local service provision. GPs can prescribe substitute or other medication.

DRUG DEPENDENCY UNITS

DDUs are often attached to hospitals. They provide counselling, detoxification, substitute prescribing and related therapies. They consist of multidisciplinary teams who work together to manage the drug users. Community drugs teams offer similar services to DDUs but are based in the community. Most drug and alcohol treatment in some areas of the country has been re-tendered in recent years. This may now be provided by major national charities and other non-profit bodies. They will no longer be managed by the NHS. Some agencies and counselling services offer alcohol-specific support.

STREET AGENCIES OR OUTREACH SERVICES

These services are designed to be accessible. They aim to reduce the harm caused by drug use, and offer services such as a needle exchange, counselling, advice and information.

PRIVATE HEALTH CARE

There are a number of private doctors and clinics who will prescribe substitute or other medication. These can be expensive, and there is a risk that users will fund the treatment by selling a proportion of the drugs if prescribing is too liberal.

MUTUAL AID

At its most simple level, mutual aid can be described as people with similar experiences helping each other to manage or overcome issues. What it implies is a system where people come together with their peers to build networks of support (Public Health England 2010). As the recovery movement progresses there are substantial recovery communities developing across the UK.

Does treatment work?

This is difficult to evaluate, as there is some evidence that people stop using alcohol/drugs over time, that is, they may 'grow out of it'. In-patient seems to be more effective than out-patient detoxification in getting users to be drug-free (81 per cent as opposed to 17 according to one study) but there is a high relapse rate. Many users go through a 'revolving door' process of detoxification followed by relapse. However, there is a very respectable body of research on natural recovery and long-term abstinence, particularly from alcohol. Research on all aspects of recovery should be understood.

Programmes that do not tackle the psychological and social aspects of alcohol/drug use are unlikely to be successful. Detoxification followed by rehabilitation and/or support services are more likely to prevent relapse. Treatment is more likely to work if the goals set are realistic; for example, stabilisation may be a more realistic prospect than 'cure' for many users.

Further information

- DrugScope: www.drugscope.org.uk

- FRANK: www.talktofrank.com

- National Treatment Agency: www.nta.nhs.uk (NTA is now part of Public Health England but retains its own dedicated website).

Recovery

In all the policies and research documents on recovery, it is seen as a process through which people are enabled to move forward to a life free of problematic substance use. It will encompass stabilisation and maintenance and for some, hopefully many, becoming abstinent. It has many pathways, including through treatment and support of self-help and mutual aid. It involves examining supports which enhance social and recovery capital and exists on a continuum of health and wellbeing. The following will contribute to the different areas of recovery:

- carers and families

- criminal justice

- education

- employment and volunteering

- housing

- recovery communities

- treatment agencies.

Recovery-Oriented Systems of Care (ROSC) are based on the principles of empowerment and choice for individuals (CSAT 2009). Stages of ROSC can be described as:

- engagement

- preparation

- change

- completion

- reintegration (runs throughout the process and marks the move-on stage).

(Tallon and Barlow 2012)

In effect, treatment agencies should be working with self-help, families and communities to support journeys of recovery (NTA 2012).

Outcomes-focused work

Recovery work is enhanced by the concept of working on outcomes:

> The definition of outcomes is the impact or end results of services on a person's life. Outcome-focused services aim to achieve the aspirations, goals and priorities identified by service users and carers – in contrast to services whose content and/or form of delivery are standardised or determined solely by those who deliver them. (Glendinning *et al.* 2008)

Work by IRISS in Scotland is useful in setting out outcome-focused work in parental problem substance use.

Children and recovery

The impetus for recovery largely hinges on work with the individual, yet we know empirically that children and young people are materially affected by their parent's recovery journey. What we do not yet know is what these effects are. As Harbin's 'roller coaster' of change (2006) illustrates, children and young people may experience very different effects from the parental journey. Moe (2008) suggests the difficulties that can commence for children when their parents enter a recovery programme. When the fabric of family life is built upon dealing with problematic substance use, the changes brought about by recovery for the parent can destabilise a child's life. Whilst this may appear counter-intuitive, that is, it is good that parents recover because children will be safer, this may not be the case. Children's emotional wellbeing is affected by a host of other factors including pre-existing 'stressors' which may be detrimental to child development and family stability (Taylor and Lazenbatt 2014). Perhaps the example of the 'parent child' is useful here. Children who have been used to taking control, monitoring the household and keeping vigilant watch over their parents, will feel the loss of this identity acutely (Barnard 2007; Radcliffe 2011):

> 'It's like I'm used to daen all the tidying up and the cooking and like telling (siblings) when to be in and who no tae hang about with and where not to go…and my mum's started daen that and it's like a kind of conflict between us now because she's like saying "you're 17, I'm the mum".' (Bancroft *et al.* 2004)

Attachment issues, neglect and trauma will not be easily ameliorated and much more research and evidence-based practice is necessary in order to support children as they experience and benefit from their parent's recovery (LTSB Foundation for Scotland Partnership Drugs Initiative – Recovery and Children Project).

Policy contexts

WORKING TOGETHER TO SAFEGUARD AND PROMOTE THE WELFARE OF CHILDREN (2015)

This updates all previous guidance and sets out the overarching responsibilities which local authorities have for safeguarding and promoting the welfare of *all* children in their area. The statutory responsibilities laid out in the 1989 and 2004 Children Acts are the legislative frameworks for the guidance (England and Wales). The key principles are:

- safeguarding is everyone's responsibility

- a child-centred approach.

Local Safeguarding Children's Boards must be established in every local authority area. The LSCB has a range of roles and statutory functions including developing local safeguarding policy and protocols and scrutinising local arrangements. Membership is set out in the guidance and the LSCB should work with the local Family Justice Board as well as the Health and Wellbeing Board, informing and designing the Joint Strategic Needs Assessment. It is not clear how significant changes in both health and social care policy in changing government administrations has affected the working of LSCBs. Alcohol and drugs policy and practice now lies within the remit of Public Health England since the subsuming of the National Treatment Agency into that body.

SERIOUS CASE REVIEWS

Unfortunately a disproportionate number of SCRs contain within them evidence of problematic parental alcohol and drug use (Brandon 2012; Ofsted 2011; Petch *et al.* 2012). Since 2013 there has been a national panel of independent experts to advise LSCBs about the initiation and publication of SCRs in England. Recent work by Adfam has highlighted a number of SCRs where the ingestion of opiate substitution medication (largely methadone) by children and young people, either accidentally or intentionally, has been the cause of the initiation of a SCR (Adfam 2014, 2015).

LOCAL FAMILY JUSTICE BOARDS – ENGLAND

These bodies were created following the Norgrove Family Justice Review in 2011. The board's responsibilities include family proceedings in both public law (e.g. care proceedings) and private law (e.g. residence/contact). Such boards have obvious relevance for children and families affected by problem alcohol and other drug use, as their objective is to drive significant improvements in the performance of the family justice system, in delivering the best possible outcomes for children. The board will require:

- credible and transparent assessment and analysis of the family prior to the issue of proceedings

- higher standard of chronologies from local authorities with reference to a full social work assessment document

- enhanced expert reports

- shorter timescales for experts to report

- enhanced communication between professionals within the family justice system.

GETTING IT RIGHT FOR EVERY CHILD – SCOTLAND

In 2008, the Scottish Government instituted Scotland's approach to supporting children and young people. Since then it has become the bedrock for all legislation, policy, practice and strategy pertaining to children and young people. It is a framework which allows all organisations and agencies who work on behalf of children and their families to provide a consistent, supportive approach to all. It encourages earlier intervention by professionals to avoid crisis situations at a later date. It provides for:

- one child, one plan

- a named person/lead professional to work on behalf of each individually assessed child

- collective responsibility.

GIRFEC is expected to be followed by all services, including those who work with adult problem alcohol and other drug users who have responsibility for children.

Care by family and friends – the legal framework

This briefing is based on advice sheets published by the Family Rights Group, who provide a range of free materials about the legal and financial aspects of kinship care. Further information is available on www.frg.org.uk.

Many children in need of permanent substitute care are placed with members of their extended family, often grandparents, or with friends. This is an alternative to being looked after in a placement provided by children's social services such as foster carers, residential care or 'stranger' adopters. Such arrangements may be known as kinship care, or family and friends placements, and are often used where parents are affected by problem drug and alcohol use.

The advantages of kinship care placements can be:

- avoidance of local authority care and being looked after by strangers

- greater stability of arrangements

- potential to maintain links with birth parents and other family members

- promotion or maintenance of a young person's racial, religious and cultural heritage.

Disadvantages can include:

- loss of freedom and independence for the carers

- practical difficulties, such as financial hardship and overcrowding

- emotional difficulties and distorted family dynamics

- continued problematic relationships with birth parents, especially around contact

- inability to access care leavers' services.

The Children and Young People Act 2014 in Scotland sets out greater involvement of kinship care and allows for support and financial arrangements.

In recent years there have been a number of important research documents which tease out some of the complexities of kinship care. The research carried out by the University of Bristol and Buttle UK (Selwyn *et al.* 2015) indicates the very substantial numbers of children affected by problem alcohol and other drug use who are looked after by kinship carers. Other work which should be considered is:

- Kroll (2007)

- Burgess *et al.* (2010).

The following are the formal and informal routes by which children can be cared for by family and friends. In some of these, the child is 'looked after' by the local authority; in others, they are not. The different routes have different implications for the decisions that the carers can make about the child, and for the support they can expect.

Private arrangements

There is no automatic local authority involvement in private arrangements made for another close family member to raise a child – although such an arrangement has no legal security. However, care by an adult who was not an immediate relative would be classed as a private fostering situation, and the local authority is required to know about these placements and to make regular visits.

FINANCIAL HELP

There is no specific help available in these circumstances, but the local authority could provide support, including cash, through s17 of the Children Act 1989. This is discretionary, and would only apply to children felt to be in need. If financial help is given under s17 it is more likely to be a one-off payment than continued support. If private foster carers receive money from the child's parents, this will be treated as income, and will affect entitlement to income support or job seeker's allowance.

Residence orders (s8, Children Act 1989)

A residence order settles the arrangements about where a child should live – and who they should live with. This might be a shared arrangement, and the person (or people) holding the order will share parental responsibility (PR)[1] with birth parent(s) or anybody else who holds PR. Residence orders generally last until a child is 16, although the Adoption and Children Act 2002 now enables the court to direct that this can be until the child reaches 18. Anybody can apply for a residence order, though most people, including relatives, will need the consent of the court beforehand. Orders are often made accompanied by a time-limited supervision order to the local authority if initial help is needed, for example in contact arrangements with birth parents. On the making of a residence order, any care

---

1   Parental responsibility is defined as 'all the rights, duties, powers, responsibilities and authority which by law a parent of a child has in relation to the child and his property'.

order or voluntary accommodation comes to an end, so a child will cease to be looked after by the local authority.

FINANCIAL HELP

The local authority can pay a residence order allowance: this is a discretionary payment which is reviewed annually. Local authorities will decide whether and how much to pay based on an assessment of the needs of the child and the financial resources of the carers. (Payment is more likely if negotiated, and confirmed in writing, prior to the child being placed.) Residence order payments will not affect child tax credit or other allowances and benefits, except housing benefit and council tax benefit. People holding a residence order should also claim child benefit.

Fostering (family placement regulations, Children Act 1989)

Family and friends can be assessed as foster carers for a specific child or children; this means they are assessed and approved by a local authority panel in the same way as other foster carers, but only to care for a specific child. This can happen before the child is placed or, if the child has gone to live with family or friends in an emergency, should take place within six weeks of the placement (s11). Assessments would look at the capacity of the carers to care for particular children. This has implications for the way in which these cases are assessed. For example, strong and supportive attachments between the child and carers may counterbalance other factors, such as accommodation, deemed important when assessing mainstream foster carers. Special consideration would also need to be paid to the issue of managing contact with birth parents in kinship placements. Children placed in this way will remain 'looked after' children, and the foster carers do not acquire PR.

FINANCIAL HELP

If the child is placed under a fostering arrangement, a fostering allowance is payable immediately. Under a 2001 court ruling known as the Munby judgement, this allowance should be the same rate as that payable to 'stranger' foster carers, irrespective of whether the arrangements are short term or long term. A foster carer cannot claim child tax credit or child benefit for that child, nor can carers claim an additional allowance for fostered children when claiming housing/council tax benefit or income support. However, fostering allowances are disregarded when calculating these two means tested benefits, as they are in claims for pension credit, job seeker's allowance, carer's allowance, widow's allowance or incapacity benefit. Fostering allowance is also ignored when calculating child tax credit, providing the amount does not exceed a certain limit (currently £10,000p.a. plus £200p.w. for each child under 11 and £250p.w. for each child over 11).

Special guardianship (s115, Adoption and Children Act 2002)

This order fits broadly in between a residence order and an adoption order in terms of the carer taking responsibility for the child. It aims to provide permanence short of adoption

– which severs all legal ties with birth family. A special guardian will have responsibility for all the day-to-day decisions about the child and their upbringing, and can exercise PR to the exclusion of any other holder. The parents of the child retain PR, but their ability to exercise this will be very limited. A special guardianship order lasts until a child is 18. It can be revoked, although the court would have to believe there had been a significant change in circumstances in order to agree to hear an application to do so. Holders of a special guardianship order will have access to a full range of support services, including financial help, counselling and mediation services, for example around contact.

FINANCIAL HELP

The local authority can pay a special guardianship allowance. This is based on a means tested assessment of the financial circumstances of the carers. Payment is discretionary unless the carer was previously a foster carer for the child. Special guardianship payments will not affect child tax credit or other allowances and benefits, except housing benefit and council tax benefit. People holding a special guardianship order should also claim child benefit.

Adoption

Kinship carers can apply to adopt. An adoption order severs all legal ties between an adopted child and their parents, although contact may still continue. Adoption creates a legal and permanent relationship between the child and the adoptive parents. Once an adoption is made, children are no longer looked after by the local authority, and the adopters hold sole parental responsibility. The Adoption and Children Act 2002 has widened the scope of prospective adopters, and any approved person or couple – who can be unmarried or same-sex couples – can now apply to be approved as adopters.

FINANCIAL HELP

Adopters may be entitled to an adoption allowance, based on the needs of the child and the family circumstances. It can often be paid in situations where it is considered that adoption would not otherwise be practical or possible. Adoption allowances are ignored when calculating entitlement to child tax credit or other allowances, except for housing benefit or council tax benefit. Working adopters may be entitled to adoption leave.

Challenges for kinship placements

Care by family and friends is rarely without some level of difficulties, and should not be regarded as an easy and cheap option for permanency, one that requires no further support. Tensions and disagreements, for example between birth parents and grandparents, about responsibilities and conflicting loyalties can quickly arise. Such tensions may be compounded by anger and worry about the parents' drug use; families may feel ashamed and guilty that birth parents are unable to care for their children, and wonder about their own role in contributing to the parents' use of drugs. They may be reluctant to ask for help for fear of being perceived as being unable to cope or through not wanting to generate further difficulties for the family.

Some professionals also find such care arrangements quite difficult, and that relationships between themselves and 'stranger' foster carers are more straightforward and easier to deal with. The family will know more about the child(ren) than the social worker, and so the power balance will be affected. The social worker may be unclear about what can reasonably be expected of the carers, or may tolerate situations and concerns that would be challenged at a much earlier stage if the carers were 'strangers'. Families themselves, whilst keen to offer a permanent home, may feel exploited and used when the extent of their responsibilities is balanced against the low level of support they may receive.

It remains the case that most children's needs are best met within their birth families, and this can be done through a variety of routes, some of which potentially bring a great deal of practical and financial support. It is important that professionals are aware of the choices available to carers, and remain mindful of their need for support.

5

Practice Examples

A letter from a paediatrician to prospective adopters

Dear Carers,

Thank you for coming to see me about Joshua; I thought it may be helpful for you to have a written record of our meeting. I understand that you are currently looking after him and hope to do so until he reaches independence. You were aware of some of his birth mother's history, and we discussed what relevance this had for Joshua.

Birth mother used a variety of street drugs throughout pregnancy, though as is often the case we do not know precisely which drugs were taken, in what combination and in what quantity. Mother was enrolled on a treatment programme which used methadone to help her reduce her opiate (heroin) use and also took prescribed medication to treat her depression. I explained that the mother had received very little antenatal care, as she found it difficult to attend hospital appointments, was not registered with a GP and moved very frequently, making it difficult for the community midwife to visit.

I explained that research on the effect of antenatal exposure to street drugs on children has not always produced clear results; one of the reasons for this is that some studies have not differentiated between the direct effect of antenatal exposure to street drugs and the influence that being brought up in a chaotic, deprived environment has had. However, I was able to give you some information which explained the symptoms that Joshua has already experienced and which could shed light on difficulties he may have in future. I explained that the street and prescribed drugs, the alcohol, cigarettes, mother's poor nutrition, psychological and physical trauma and infections were likely to have had a cumulatively adverse effect upon Joshua, and that it would not be possible to attribute any difficulties he may experience to a specific cause.

We are aware that the mother injected heroin throughout pregnancy; she denied sharing needles, but may have done so, particularly during the time she spent in prison. Mother's heroin use may have contributed to Joshua's small weight for his gestational age and his decreased head size, but these features are also associated with cigarette smoking and poor nutrition, etc. When he was born Joshua required no resuscitation, but about 24 hours after birth he became very irritable, was difficult to feed and was very 'jittery', i.e. his movements were very jerky; he also developed a fever and diarrhoea which caused him to have a very sore bottom. He had some difficulty with his breathing. He had two brief seizures (fits) on his third day. Joshua was unfortunate in suffering most of the symptoms of neonatal abstinence (withdrawal) syndrome. Such symptoms, which can last from a few days to several months, mostly appear in the first 24–72 hours after birth, but they can be delayed for up to five weeks. Joshua was nursed on the neonatal unit so that he could be given some support with his breathing; he was tube fed for five days but gradually his sucking and swallowing became more organised and he was able to bottle feed. I understand that he is still a difficult little boy to feed, but the community neonatal nurse and health visitor have given you advice about different teats, milk formulae, etc. I am pleased that his sore bottom is now recovering following the use of Metanium cream.

As Joshua's withdrawal symptoms were quite severe, he was given Oramorph (morphine sulphate), with the dose being altered in response to his symptoms, which were monitored by scoring on a chart, one point being given for each symptom (e.g. sneezing, irritability, jittering) to a maximum of ten. You also used this chart to help you and the neonatal nurse to decide how quickly to reduce his Oramorph once he came home. Joshua has stopped taking Oramorph about seven days ago, but he is still requiring chloral sometimes when he is irritable and you have also found that wrapping him up in a cotton sheet and holding him close to you has helped. I explained that I would expect Joshua's symptoms gradually to improve, though this may take several months.

The neonatal unit has explained that the abnormal breathing patterns which can occur with neonatal abstinence syndrome may persist for up to three weeks; these *may* be associated with an increased incidence of sudden infant death syndrome, but this is not certain. In any case you were already following the guidelines of putting Joshua to sleep on his back, making sure he was not too hot at night and not exposing him to any cigarette smoke.

We acknowledged that the mother had also taken methadone as part of her treatment programme – withdrawal from this is likely to have contributed to Joshua's symptoms. Moreover, as methadone takes longer to clear from the body it is likely to make withdrawal symptoms persist for longer.

I explained that the other drugs that the mother may have used can also cause similar symptoms in babies to heroin withdrawal. The toxic effect of cocaine can include sleep disturbance, poor suck, vomiting, soft stools, irritability and occasionally a condition called necrotising enterocolitis, which causes severe inflammation of the lining of the intestine. Neonates withdrawing from amphetamines may experience jitteriness, drowsiness and respiratory distress. Babies exposed to a lot of cannabis may have symptoms such as tremor and an exaggerated response to sudden events, e.g. a loud noise. We acknowledged that sudden infant death syndrome is significantly greater in children exposed to cocaine and amphetamines.

We also know that the mother had taken temazepam (one of the benzodiazepine group), commonly used to reduce anxiety or as a sedative. These drugs are concentrated in the developing baby and may take a long time to clear from the baby's system. Affected babies can be very sleepy, floppy and have difficulties in sucking; they may also have brief periods of apnoea (cessation of breathing), cyanosis and difficulty in maintaining their body temperature at a high enough level. Less frequently muscle tone is increased and the babies feel stiff. These symptoms may persist for several months. Fortunately Joshua does not appear to have these symptoms.

I explained that examination of Joshua had not revealed any abnormalities, though he was rather small for his gestational age. There is some research which suggests that exposure to cocaine in particular can cause babies to have some particular facial features and a small head. Although research is not absolutely conclusive, children exposed to ecstasy, particularly in a repeated way, may be at increased risk of having heart defects and problems with their muscles and bones. There is no conclusive evidence that the other commonly used street drugs cause structural abnormalities.

Mother took an antidepressant intermittently during the pregnancy. This too may have contributed to Joshua's symptoms of jitteriness, irritability and seizures. Also there is a possibility that babies who have had recent exposure to fluoxetine (Prozac) may be more likely to bleed, and therefore of course you should seek urgent medical advice if Joshua has any abnormal bleeding or bruising in the next few weeks.

We then went on to discuss what possible long-term effects Joshua's exposure to this variety of street drugs may have. Research has produced conflicting results, and more is needed, but evidence indicates that some children exposed to street drugs may have attention deficit, below average coordination skills and other learning disorders. As Joshua is just four weeks old, only very significant developmental disorders would be apparent and we have to wait until he is of the appropriate age before we can say that he will develop speech and language, fine motor skills, etc. This principle also applies to his personality and behaviour.

We know that the mother was a heavy cigarette smoker throughout pregnancy. This is likely to increase Joshua's risk of having sensitive airways, which means that his airways are more likely to narrow in response to an upper respiratory infection, e.g. a cold or if he is exposed to tobacco smoke; later this narrowing may occur during exercise or at night. Symptoms of wheeze or any cough which persists after a cold, reduces exercise tolerance or wakes Joshua at night should be discussed with his GP. Of course he should not be exposed to tobacco smoke and strongly discouraged from smoking himself.

Unfortunately the birth mother was not tested for the blood-borne viruses hepatitis B, hepatitis C and HIV in pregnancy; as she continued to inject and had a variety of sexual partners she was at risk of contracting any of these infections. I explained that Joshua and his mum could be infected without showing any signs or symptoms of illness, and therefore only appropriate blood testing can establish or rule out infection. I therefore recommended that we took some blood from Joshua to establish his viral status, and depending on the test performed, we may be able to reassure you that he was negative and therefore would not develop any of the diseases. A positive antibody test would indicate that either the mother's antibodies had crossed the placenta or that Joshua is infected, and therefore further testing would be necessary. It is to Joshua's advantage to know if he is infected, as then monitoring of the condition and appropriate treatment could substantially improve his quality of life and longevity.

You asked whether Joshua was likely to become a street drug user like his mother. There is some evidence from twin and adoption studies that there is a genetic component to alcohol abuse, but it is known that environmental factors play a significant part in the development of such behaviour too. I therefore recommended that Joshua should have excellent health education in respect of substance misuse, that he should have good role models of sensible drinking, and that you should be very open to discussing all relevant topics with him as he grows.

In conclusion we agreed that Joshua is a delightful little boy who has not had the best start in life with his exposure to an unknown variety of street drugs, cigarettes and alcohol and his birth mother's poor nutrition and trauma. He received appropriate treatment and care in the neonatal unit, but was looked after by his birth mother and a variety of nurses, and has therefore had changes in principal carer which is detrimental to his attachment formation. Joshua has experienced a number of difficulties, particularly with irritability and feeding, which are resolving, but it is important that you continue to seek support from the community neonatal nurse, health visitor and other health and social service professionals when necessary, not only asking for advice about Joshua's specific problems but also for support for yourselves if you were having a lot of sleepless nights, experiencing frustration in feeding him, etc.

Joshua may experience developmental and behavioural difficulties as he grows; he should have all the routine health and developmental assessments with any identified problems being individually assessed and managed. He is likely to benefit from a structured nursery at the appropriate time, but may also need therapeutic input from speech and language therapists, physiotherapists and occupational therapists in addition to the educational psychology service if he has learning problems. Behaviourally Joshua and you may need support from psychological services, and these should preferably be delivered by professionals experienced in the particular emotional needs of children who have been looked after. If you would like more information about these issues the book *Children Exposed to Parental Substance Misuse*, published by BAAF, is most helpful.

I hope you feel this covers our discussions. Please do not hesitate to be in touch if you want clarification of any of the points or further information.

Yours sincerely,

Medical Adviser, Fostering and Adoption

Sample core assessment

It is important that core assessments not only capture essential information but provide the basis for planning, intervention and review. This is not always the case. For example, 'X needs a loving and secure attachment in which to fulfil her potential' indicates nothing about the particular needs of X living with parents whose drug use is adversely affecting their parenting capacity and, being a universal need, would apply to any child in any circumstances.

By way of a guide, we have included the final part of a fictitious core assessment for a child affected by parental drug misuse.

Aimee

This is a fictitious assessment about Aimee, a six-year-old black British child who lives with her mother, Ms Spencer, a single parent with a four-year history of poly-drug use which includes both crack cocaine and heroin. Aimee has recently been placed on the Child Protection Register because of mounting concerns about her poor home circumstances and neglect. These are felt to be a direct result of her mother's drug use and attendant chaotic lifestyle. Children's social services has a history of referrals concerning the neglect of Aimee and, latterly, of requests for s17 (financial) assistance from Ms Spencer. Individually the referrals were not serious, but over time presented a worrying picture. S47 (child protection) enquiries were begun following a referral from Aimee's school about her poor attendance, lateness, unkempt appearance and Aimee's disclosure to her teacher that she sees her mother injecting.

Ms Spencer has been intermittently cooperative with social services but was reluctant to talk about her drug use, and keen to minimise both the extent of it and the impact upon her ability to care for Aimee. She has been in treatment in the past, but was discharged after less than a month for non-compliance. She is not currently in treatment and has little enthusiasm for pursuing this.

Analysis of the information gathered during the core assessment

The analysis should list the factors that have an impact on different aspects of the child's development and parenting capacity, and explore the relationship between them. This process of analysing the information available about the child's needs, parenting capacity and family and environmental factors should result in a clear understanding of the child's needs, and what types of service provision would best address these needs to ensure the child has the opportunity to achieve their potential.

Aimee presents as an anxious, guarded and isolated child who is worried about her mother and reluctant to say much about her home life; this may be because she has been instructed to do so, or it may be an emerging sense of the poverty of her home life and a growing awareness of the difference between her circumstances and those of other children at school. Ms Spencer insists that Aimee knows nothing about her drug use. This is clearly not the case, as Aimee has described seeing her mother inject and is aware of the pejorative comments of neighbours.

Aimee has little routine at home – a feature of her mother's chaotic lifestyle. This leads to her being tired during school hours and frequently late. She is a bright girl, of above average intelligence, whose progress is being hampered by her mother's inability to afford sufficient priority to Aimee's education needs. Aimee has also missed a great deal of school, particularly in the period coinciding with her mother's absence through imprisonment. Aimee suffers from a lack of stimulation – she has spoken of being frequently left to her own devices – and impaired concentration and attainment. These are directly attributable to her mother's lifestyle and unavailability, the results of poly-drug use.

Aimee presents with a maturity far beyond that of her chronological age. This may be a result of her mother's unavailability and preoccupation, and by pressures to grow up fast and to assume increasing adult responsibilities. Aimee not only carries too much responsibility for her own care (attending to her own hygiene and some of her own meals), she also provides a level of care and support to her mother, whom she describes as being 'ill' at times. Aimee may be on the edge of being deemed to be a young carer, which, at the age of six, is highly inappropriate.

Ms Spencer's use of illicit drugs has led to a range of practical and emotional consequences – all of which have adversely impacted on Aimee's life, or on her ability to care for Aimee.

On a practical level, Aimee lives in very impoverished circumstances which are unhygienic and 'barely good enough' in terms of safety. The family risk being made homeless, and are the subject of sustained hostility from neighbours because of disturbances by visitors. Ms Spencer may not be able to control what happens in the home, and Aimee risks being exposed to drug-using activity, to witnessing violence or being accidentally injured. Aimee is allowed to play unsupervised outdoors, which renders her highly vulnerable, and is frequently cared for by other adults who are themselves drug users.

Emotionally Aimee will experience her mother as being volatile and unreliable. Ms Spencer's use of heroin would cause her to become drowsy, relaxed and unavailable, whereas the stimulant effects of crack cocaine may cause her to be inappropriately euphoric or disinhibited. Opiate withdrawal is physically unpleasant and would cause Ms Spencer to appear ill in a way that would be very frightening for a young child. Her relationship with her mother is likely to be one of anxiety and worry on the part of Aimee – with an increasing need to try and take control for her mother and assume a level of responsibility for her.

There is no alternative adult, or other robust family support, to compensate Aimee for her mother's difficulties, the effects of which are likely to be cumulative. Ms Spencer has refused to give permission for discussion with her extended family – or indeed the information to allow such discussions to take place.

Aimee's needs are neglected at many levels. At the moment she has adapted by becoming inappropriately adult and well behaved – but as Aimee approaches adolescence she may find different sorts of behaviours to replace these. She is 'losing' her childhood and has diminishing life chances in terms of future educational attainment. Her sense of self-worth and importance is very low and may render her vulnerable to abusive relationships in the future.

In the absence of Ms Spencer addressing her drug use, direct services to Aimee will be of limited use and their benefits will be undermined by her mother's continued behaviour, which poses a risk to Aimee's development. Ms Spencer is keen to minimise both the amount and the impact of her drug use, and appears to have little enthusiasm for either treatment and stabilisation or for abstinence. Should the situation remain unchanged, it can be predicted that a series of crises are likely to occur, possibly an arrest or an episode of violence, or Aimee being found unattended at home, such that the local authority will be compelled to take action to address the immediate situation and ensure Aimee's safety. Aimee risks entering the care system because of such a crisis. The mandate of the child protection plan has so far not effected any change in Ms Spencer's ability to work with professionals, and she failed to attend a recent core group whose task was to draw up a detailed protection plan.

To achieve this, her mother needs to stop using drugs or to comply with a treatment programme such that her drug use no longer affects her parenting. Aimee needs to know that she is, demonstrably, more important to her mother than use of drugs: that her mother's primary attachment is to her and not to heroin and crack cocaine. Aimee needs to attend school regularly and on time, and for an adult to have oversight of her daily care. Ms Spencer needs to be supported in these tasks. This includes help in rendering the accommodation safer and more suitable, and assistance and support in budgeting and literacy. Aimee also needs to stop being a young carer and having such inappropriate responsibility for her mother. She needs to know that her mother's drug use is not her fault, that she can't control her mother and that she can't cure her. Aimee would benefit from the opportunity to form a relationship with a trusted adult where she can express some of her worries and concerns and receive information about drug use that is factual, age-appropriate and non-judgemental. Aimee needs to be allowed to be a child, with normal friendships and a lifestyle that does not single her out as being different from other children.

The existing core group should meet with Ms Spencer as a matter of urgency, to draw up with her a very comprehensive, and time-limited, programme about expectations of future involvement and change. Of these expectations, a commitment to enter into treatment, and to comply with that treatment, must be the most important. If there is no demonstrable improvement in Aimee's circumstances within a relatively short time period – a maximum of six weeks – then discussion should take place with the local authority legal team about the value and timing of an application to court to enable the local authority to share parental responsibility for Aimee with her mother.

Decisions following the core assessment (tick as appropriate)

Initiate a strategy discussion	☐	Provision of services (s17)	☐
Immediate legal action to protect the child	☐	Referral to other agency(ies)	☐
Commission a specialist assessment(s)	☐	Other (please specify) _____ Legal planning meeting to discuss need for legal action	☐
Provide accommodation (including respite care)	☐	No further action	☐

The experiences of a parental substance misuse and child care social worker
Job description

The following is a description of a specialist post created by Islington Children's Services/ Mental Health and Social Care Trust, to improve the service for substance-misusing parents and their children.

Aims of the post

To provide social worker expertise within a pilot development in the borough which will lead on to the delivery and development of cross-agency care packages to substance-misusing parents and their children. The post holder will work alongside a substance misuse and child care health lead. Together they will work with social services, primary and secondary health care services and statutory and voluntary drug and alcohol agencies to develop clear pathways of care and support for children of substance misusers, with the ultimate aim of promoting and improving the health and wellbeing of these children and young people. This will involve a combination of individual and group casework with drug and alcohol users who are parents, and working closely with the services involved in their treatment.

Duties and responsibilities

1. To develop clear pathways of care between statutory and voluntary sector substance misuse services and social care and primary care services, ensuring each child has a multi-agency plan.

2. To increase the number of children of drug-using parents accessing appropriate health care including developmental checks.

3. To provide advice, information and training to social services staff working with children of substance-misusing parents and to provide advice, information and training to statutory and voluntary sector substance misuse services around working with substance misusers who are parents, including their responsibilities when working with this client group.

4. To work with the local obstetric departments to ensure the problem drug and alcohol use by pregnant women is routinely recorded at antenatal clinics and to forge links that will enable them to respond in a coordinated way to the needs of the children of problem drug users and to monitor the numbers of births of problem drug and alcohol users recorded for the borough from local hospitals.

5. To raise awareness about and review as appropriate the protocols that exist between drug and alcohol services and child protection services and to lead on ensuring that specialist drug and alcohol services ask and record the number, age and whereabouts of all clients' children in a consistent manner.

6. To work with children and family social work services in their work with children of problem drug and alcohol users for an integrated approach based on a Common Assessment Framework.

7. To screen the needs of children whose parents are problem drug and alcohol users, completing an initial assessment where required.

8. To work closely with the specialist substance misuse and parenting health care post and share work appropriately.

9. To carry a caseload of child in need cases, assessing need, contributing to the formulation of plans for children, implementing and contributing to reviews of those plans, and carrying out such tasks as may be necessary to do so. To undertake and coordinate assessments of children who may be deemed to be in need and identify, coordinate and/or provide an appropriate package of care.

10. To convene, chair and/or attend professional meetings and family support meetings and participate in planning for continued support for families in partnership with other agencies. To attend and contribute to a variety of other meetings as required: these may include strategy meetings, case review conferences, working parties and training courses as required.

11. To undertake any other tasks required that help with the development of the service.

Reflections six months into post

GILL WATSON OFFERS REFLECTIONS AFTER SIX MONTHS IN POST

When I started in post I was completely overwhelmed by the scale of the task and found it difficult to know where to start. It seemed as though I was being asked to ensure that all the recommendations of *Hidden Harm* were implemented in my borough – me, a mere practitioner, not a manager or project officer!

Initially I spent a lot of time brainstorming, trying to tease out the different elements of the job description and design a work plan that would address the various requirements. It struck me that I was being asked to work on a strategic level while at the same time holding a caseload. Fortunately my steering group, comprising managers from the PCT, children's services and substance misuse services, recognised this as well, and allowed me the autonomy to prioritise the work so that the structural and procedural foundations could be laid before I got inundated with referrals.

I decided that it would be important to establish a baseline for the work I was going to do, so conducted a needs assessment that included quantitative as well as qualitative research across the three main service areas I saw myself working alongside: children's services, maternity services and substance misuse services. I wanted to find out how many families affected by substance misuse were already known to one or more agency, and how these agencies were currently working together (or not). I also felt that it was important to gauge the levels of knowledge, skills and experience that practitioners had in working with this client group, to identify training needs.

Six months down the track and I have established referral and care pathways between the three services areas, accompanied by clear flowcharts and eligibility criteria, with the aim of making 'working together' something real. I am about to start a series of training sessions across statutory children's services that will bring social workers, deputy managers, team managers and child protection coordinators up to date with current guidance and research findings, as well as ensure they have a working knowledge of the local treatment and support resources for substance users. I am also running a session for midwives in conjunction with the hospital liaison nurse from one of the treatment services, as part of their bi-monthly child protection study days.

The health visitor mentioned in my job description still hasn't been appointed, but once they are in post there is scope for better links with the child health professionals. A new family service provided by a voluntary sector organisation has also recently started, and together we plan to hold a conference in a few months' time to launch the *Hidden Harm* agenda across the borough.

My advice to anyone starting out in a similar post is never underestimate the importance of networking and research. If you don't know how things currently work, or who is doing what, how can you decide what needs changing and who to engage in the change process? The first few months might seem slow moving, with little to show, but this work bears the fruit of excellent working relationships across professional and agency boundaries, with the clients ultimately benefiting from true partnership working.

A model of multi-agency working

This is reproduced with permission from *Practitioner Toolkit: Getting It Right for Children and Families Affected by Parental Problem Alcohol and Drug Use*, on behalf of Edinburgh and Lothians Partner Agencies 2014.

SUMMARY OF PATHWAYS

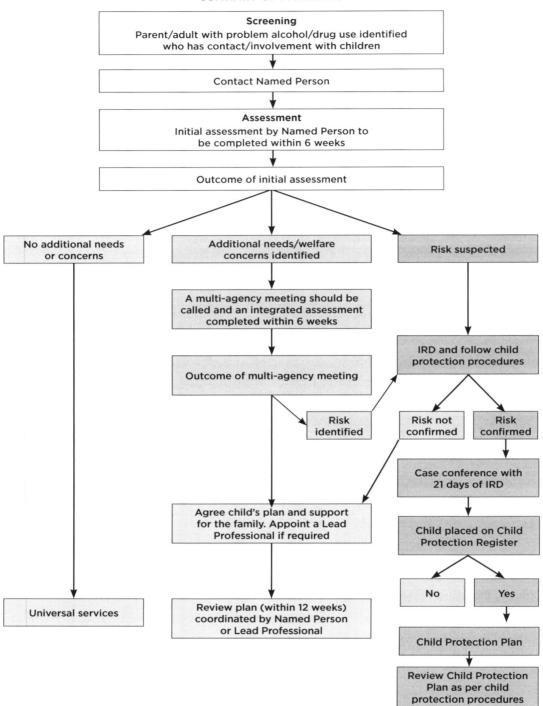

Innovative practice
Option 2 Cardiff

An intervention programme aimed at keeping together families where there are child protection concerns related to drug or alcohol misuse or where the children are at risk of becoming looked after because of these concerns. The service works intensively with families building parental skills and resilience and helping the parents create safe environments for the children.

Further information on 029 2039 8181.

Family Environment: Drug-Using Parents (FEDUP)

Helps children and parents where one or both parents misuse drugs or alcohol. It is based on a programme originally developed by NSPCC in Grimsby. It gives children aged between five and 12 a safe, confidential space to express their feelings and build self-esteem.

FEDUP helps parents understand how their children are affected by their drug or alcohol problems. It can help them reduce the effect on their children. It is available in Blackpool, Coventry and Cardiff.

Further information on the NSPCC website: www.nspcc.org.uk/services-and-resources/services-for-children-and-families/family-environment-drug-using-parents-fedup.

CASA Family Service

This has grown out of the work of CASA, a voluntary sector alcohol and drug service based in North London, helping children, young people and families who are affected by parental alcohol or drug use.

Further information on 020 7561 7490 or http://blenheimcdp.org.uk/services/casa-family.

Aberlour Child Care Trust, Glasgow, Edinburgh and Dundee

The Aberlour Trust runs a number of projects in Scotland to provide services for children whose mothers are affected by drug or alcohol use. These services are delivered on an outreach basis in the community.

Further information on 01786 450355.

Kith n Kin

This service is provided by Tayside Council on Alcohol, in partnership with the Aberlour Child Care Trust. It works alongside Kinship Care families in Dundee and Perth and Kinross. The service includes low level advice, information, brief support signposting and family based activities. It also offers more intensive one-to-one support for children and their carers, art and play therapy for children, and regular weekly groups for both children and their carers.

Further information on 01382 456012.

Creative Therapies

This organisation has been in existence since 1996, providing art, music and drama therapies within a wider arts project involving professional artists, musicians and dancers. Beneficiaries are those children and young people with emotional, physical and mental health issues, often as a result of life-threatening illness, deprivation and/or exposure to alcohol and drug misuse in the home. In 2013, as the result of a grant from the Lloyds TSB Partnership Drugs Initiative, it began to provide therapeutic arts services to children in Kinship care in the Northwest of Glasgow.

> Further information on 0141 342 4444.

Family Drug and Alcohol Court, London

Based on a model widely used across the USA, this initiative has established a model of a specialist court working within the framework of care proceedings. It uses the authority of the court to motivate and support parents while keeping the child at the centre of concern. By the use of a dedicated team to provide speedy assessment and referral, and court involvement at an earlier stage than would normally happen, more effective work can be undertaken with parents, and less delay in decision making for children. The emphasis is on working intensively with parents at an earlier stage and not simply assessing them.

> Further information on www.coram.org.uk/supporting-parents/family-drug-and-alcohol-court.

M-PACT (Moving Parents and Children Together)

A programme developed by Action on Addiction which is now available under licence, it is best described as a psychosocial and educational brief intervention that takes a whole family approach. Each programme works with up to eight families. It provides approximately ten sessions for families with children aged eight to 17, and includes:

- individual family assessment
- two-and-a-half-hour core sessions, child and parent/child and parent separately/ family support
- a family review session to make future plans.

This approach reduces feelings of isolation and encourages the process of identification and the building of informal networks of support with people with similar problems.

COAP

An online community for young people living with a family member's dependency on drugs, alcohol and gambling.

> Further information on M-PACT and COAP on www.actiononaddiction.org.uk.

Parents Under Pressure (PUP) – Promoting a nurturing environment for families

This programme has been initiated in the UK by NSPCC along with its originator Professor Sharon Dawe from Australia. It is sited in ten sites across the UK, and is home-based and combines psychological principles relating to parenting, child behaviour and parental emotion regulation with a case management model. It is highly individualised to suit each family. It is now being evaluated as an intervention with families affected by problem alcohol and other drug use. Its evaluation is ongoing.

Further information on the NSPCC website: www.nspcc.org.uk/services-and-resources/services-for-children-and-families/parents-under-pressure.

Steps to Cope

This is an adaptation of the 5-Step Method devised for the support of adult family members affected by alcohol and drug problems. It is a support programme for young people affected by parental substance misuse and/or parental mental health (Templeton 2012).

More information on www.ascert.biz.

Contacts and Sources of Further Information

ADFAM

Information, advice, counselling. National helpline for families and friends of drug users.

www.adfam.org.uk
Helpline: 020 7928 8898

ALCOHOL FOCUS SCOTLAND

The website includes details of local services and resources.

www.alcohol-focus-scotland.org.uk

BRITISH ASSOCIATION FOR ADOPTION AND FOSTERING

Information, advice, publications, training and consultancy on all aspects of family placement practice.

www.corambaaf.org.uk
Tel.: 020 7421 2600

DRUGSCOPE – NOW A LEGACY SITE

Information on drugs, library, news, services directory.

www.drugscope.org.uk

FAMILIES ANONYMOUS

Advice and support groups for families and friends.

www.familiesanonymous.org
Helpline: 0845 1200 6600

FAMILY RIGHTS GROUP

Independent advice and support for families whose children are involved with social services. Advice sheets about the legal and financial aspects of substitute care within the family.

www.frg.org.uk
Advice line: 0800 731 1696, www.advice@frg.org.uk

FRANK

Drug advice for young people.

www.talktofrank.com
Tel.: 0800 776600

HIDDEN HARM (ADVISORY COUNCIL ON THE MISUSE OF DRUGS)

www.gov.uk/government/policies/drug-misuse-and-dependency

LIFELINE

Produces a range of publications about drugs and drug use specifically aimed at the South Asian community. Materials are available in Urdu and Bengali.

www.lifeline.org.uk
Tel.: 0161 839 2075

NATIONAL DRUGS HELPLINE

Free information, advice and support around drug issues.

Tel.: 0800 776600

NATIONAL TREATMENT AGENCY

www.nta.nhs.uk

Tel.: 020 7972 2226

PRINCESS ROYAL TRUST FOR CARERS AND THE CHILDREN'S SOCIETY

Supporting Young Carers: A Resource for Schools. This includes a chapter on supporting pupils with parents affected by parental substance misuse.

Free download: http://professionals.carers.org/young-carers-and-school

SUBSTANCE MISUSE MANAGEMENT IN GENERAL PRACTICE (SMMGP)

A network to support GPs and other members of the primary health care team who work with substance misuse.

www.smmgp.co.uk

LEAFLETS AND REPORTS

Adfam produces a number of resources for children and family members and professionals.

www.adfam.org.uk or email publications@adfam.org.uk

Policies, guidelines and useful tools

We Count Too (Second edition 2009), Good Practice Guide and Quality Standards for work with family members affected by someone else's drug use. This guide provides guidance on the types of services which families need. Produced following in-depth research and consultation with family members.

www.adfam.org.uk/professionals/reference_and research/adfam_publications

Getting Our Priorities Right. Updated good practice guidance for all agencies and practitioners working with children, young people and families affected by problematic alcohol and/ or drug use. Published by the Scottish Government.

www.gov.scot/Publications/2013/04/2305

PDI Briefing Paper 01, *Understanding What Makes a Good Project.*

www.ltsbfoundationforscotland.org.uk/documents/PDI%20Briefing%20Paper%2001%20 -%20What%20makes%20a%20good%20project.pdf

SCIE Resource Guide 2, *Families That Have Alcohol and Mental Health Problems: A Template for Partnership Working.* June 2003.

www.scie.org.uk/publications/guides/guide02

STARS project. The Children's Society's STARS project in Nottingham is dedicated to providing assistance to children who have been impacted by a parent's substance misuse. It offers a therapeutic relationship, and aims to build resilience in the child and to strengthen their coping strategies.

www.childrenssociety.org.uk

Stella Project. Toolkit relating to domestic violence, drugs and alcohol: good practice guidelines. *AVA (Against Violence and Abuse)* (Second edition 2007).

www.avaproject.org.uk

In 2010 the National Treatment Agency and Government Departments produced guidelines to develop joint protocols for working with children and families affected by substance misuse.

www.nta.nhs.uk

A number of local authorities have also produced guidelines to support professionals working with children and families where parental drug use is affecting care of the children:

City & Hackney Safeguarding Children's Board and Hackney Drug Action Team (2006) *Joint Protocol between Hackney Drug Action Team and Children's Social Care.*

Resources for direct work with children affected by parental alcohol and other drug use

STARS project has produced a wide range of materials for direct work with children.

www.starsnationalinitiative.org.uk

Can You See the Elephant?, a course for those working with children affected by a parent/ carer's drug use, was produced by Leicestershire Healthy Schools Team 05/06.

Explores how parenting capacity may be compromised and how children may be affected by parental substance misuse.

Referred to in SCIE e-learning resource, *Parental Substance Misuse – Module 1: Understanding the impact on children* (2011), www.scie.org.uk/publications/elearning/parentalsubstancemisuse

Adfam has produced a publication *When Parents Take Drugs* for use by anyone talking with young people about a parent or carer's drug use. It is aimed at a wide audience including teachers, youth workers and health professionals. It contains scenarios or prompts to help young people think about the issues, together with suggestions to adults about how discussion might be facilitated.

www.adfam.org.uk

Alcohol Focus Scotland has produced two resources to help children understand parental alcohol misuse. *Rory* is aimed at primary school children and has been evaluated (AFS 2012). *Oh Lila* is produced for 3–5-year-olds.

www.alcohol-focus-scotland.org.uk/training/working-with-children-and-young-people

Essential reading

Aberlour Child Care Trust (2007) *A Matter of Substance? Alcohol or Drugs: Does It Make a Difference to the Child?* Available at www.aberlour.org.uk/assets/0001/0361/TT2_A_Matter_of_Substance_Report.pdf, accessed on 9 February 2016.

Adamson, J., and Templeton, L. (2012) *Silent Voices: Supporting Children and Young People Affected by Parental Alcohol Misuse.* London: Office of the Children's Commissioner, Community Research Company.

Advisory Council on the Misuse of Drugs (2003) *Hidden Harm: Responding to the Needs of Children of Problem Drug Users: The Report of an Inquiry by the Advisory Council on the Misuse of Drugs.* London: Home Office.

Advisory Council on the Misuse of Drugs (2007) *Hidden Harm Three Years On: Realities, Challenges and Opportunities.* London: Home Office.

Bancroft, A., Wilson, S., Cunningham-Burley, S., Backett-Milburn, K., and Masters, H. (2004) *Parental Drug and Alcohol Misuse: Resilience and Transition Among Young People.* York: Joseph Rowntree Foundation.

Barnard, M., and Barlow, J. (2003) 'Discovering parental drug dependence: silence and disclosure.' *Children & Society 17*, 1, 45–56.

Centre for Learning in Child Protection (2011) *Get to Know Us: Children and Young People Affected by Parents Who Misuse Alcohol. Getting It Right for Every Family.* Edinburgh: NSPCC, University of Edinburgh.

Centre for Research on Families and Relationships (2014) *Parenting Support for Mothers and Fathers with a Drug Problem. Challenges for Parents and Health Care Professionals.* Edinburgh: University of Edinburgh.

Dawe, S., *et al.* (2008) *Improving Outcomes for Children Living in Families with Substance Misuse. What Do We Know and What Should We Do?* Australian Institute of Family Studies. Available at https://aifs.gov.au/cfca/publications/improving-outcomes-children-living-families-pare, accessed on 9 February 2016.

Forrester, D., *et al.* (2008) 'Communication skills in child protection: how do social workers talk to parents?' *Child and Family Social Work 13*, 1, 41–51.

FRANK (2005) *Resources Needed to Support Children of Problematic Users of Drugs.* London: COI Communications and Home Office.

Harbin, F., and Murphy, M. (2006) *Secret Lives: Growing with Substance: Working with Children and Young People Affected by Familial Substance Misuse.* Lyme Regis: Russell House Publishing.

Harwin, J. (2010) 'Applying the 5-step method to children and families and substance misuse. Opportunities and challenges within policy and practice.' *Drugs Education, Prevention and Policy 17*, 51, 179–192.

Kearney, J., Harbin, F., Murphy, M., Wheeler, E., and Whittle, J. (2005) *The Highs and Lows of Family Life: Familial Substance Misuse from a Child's Perspective.* Bolton: Bolton Substance Misuse Research Group.

Kroll, B. (2004) 'Living with an elephant: growing up with parental substance misuse.' *Child and Family Social Work 9*, 129–140.

Kroll, B., and Taylor, A. (2008) *The Impact of Parental Substance Misuse in Child Development.* Research in Practice/Frontline. www.rip.org.uk.

Phillips, R. (ed.) (2004) *Children Exposed to Parental Substance Misuse: Implications for Family Placement.* London: BAAF.

Public Health England (2015) *Local Initiatives in Safeguarding, Sheffield and Lewisham: Safeguarding and Substance Misuse.*

Radcliffe, P. (2011) 'Motherhood, pregnancy and the negotiation of identity: the moral career of drug treatment.' *Social Science and Medicine 72,* 6, 984–991.

References

Aberlour Child Care Trust (2007) *A Matter of Substance? Alcohol or Drugs: Does It Make a Difference to the Child?* Available at www.aberlour.org.uk/assets/0001/0361/TT2_A_Matter_of_Substance_Report.pdf, accessed on 9 February 2016.

Adamson, J., and Templeton, L. (2012) *Silent Voices: Supporting Children and Young People Affected by Parental Alcohol Misuse.* London: Office of the Children's Commissioner, Community Research Company.

Adfam (2014) *Medications in Drug Treatment: Tackling the Risks to Children.* Available at www.adfam.org.uk/cms/docs/adfam_ost_fullreport_web.pdf, accessed on 10 February 2016.

Adfam (2015) *Medications in Drug Treatment: Tackling the Risks to Children – One Year On.* Available at www.adfam.org.uk/cms/docs/ost_oneyearon_full.pdf, accessed on 10 February 2016.

Advisory Council on the Misuse of Drugs (2003) *Hidden Harm: Responding to the Needs of Children of Problem Drug Users: The Report of an Inquiry by the Advisory Council on the Misuse of Drugs.* London: Home Office.

Advisory Council on the Misuse of Drugs (2007) *Hidden Harm Three Years On: Realities, Challenges and Opportunities.* London: Home Office.

AFS, NHS Greater Glasgow and Clyde, West Lothian Alcohol and Drug Partnership TASC Agency. (2012) *Evaluation of the Rory Resource.*

Alcohol Concern (2009) *Knowledge Set 2. Children and Parenting.* Embrace Project.

Allen, G., MP (2011) *Early Intervention: The Next Steps.* An Independent Report to HM Government. Available at www.gov.uk/government/uploads/system/uploads/attachment_data/file/284086/early-intervention-next-steps2.pdf, accessed on 10 February 2016.

Altshuler, S. (2005) 'Drug-endangered children need a collaborative community response.' *Child Welfare 84,* 2, 171–190.

Angus Council (n.d.) *The Wellbeing Wheel.* Available at https://archive.angus.gov.uk/girfec/well-being-wheel.html, accessed on 10 February 2016.

Bancroft, A., Wilson, S., Cunningham-Burley, S., Backett-Milburn, K., and Masters, H. (2004) *Parental Drug and Alcohol Misuse: Resilience and Transition Among Young People.* York: Joseph Rowntree Foundation.

Bancroft, A. *et al.* (2010) 'Drugs, Intoxication and Society.' *Sociology 44,* 6,1215–1217.

Barlow, J. (ed.) (2010) *Substance Misuse. The Implications of Research, Policy and Practice.* Research Highlights in Social Work 53. London: Jessica Kingsley Publishers.

Barlow, J. (2011) *Evidence Base: Parental Alcohol Misuse.* Community Care Online. Available at www.communitycare.co.uk/2011/06/16/evidence-base-parental-alcohol-misuse, accessed on 10 February 2016.

Barnard, M. (2003) 'Between a rock and a hard place: the role of relatives in protecting children from the effects of parental drug problems.' *Child and Family Social Work* 8, 291–299.

Barnard, M. (2005) *Drugs in the Family: The Impact on Parents and Siblings.* York: Joseph Rowntree Foundation.

Barnard, M. (2007) *Drug Addiction and Families.* London. Jessica Kingsley Publishers.

Barnard, M., and Barlow, J. (2003) 'Discovering parental drug dependence: silence and disclosure.' *Children & Society 17,* 1, 45–56.

Beaumont, B. (ed.) (2004) *Care of Drug Users in General Practice: A Harm Reduction Approach.* London: RCGP/Radcliffe Publishing.

Betty Ford Institute (2007) 'What is recovery? A working definition from The Betty Ford Consensus Panel.' *Journal of Substance Abuse Treatment 33,* 221–228.

BMA (2007) *Preventing and Managing Fetal Alcohol Spectrum Disorders.* Updated 2016. London: British Medical Association.

Brandon, M. *et al.* (2008). 'Analysing child deaths and serious injury through abuse and neglect: What can we learn?' *Research Report DSCF RRO 23.* Nottingham: DCSF Publications.

Brandon, M., *et al.* (2009) *Understanding Serious Case Reviews and Their Impact: A Biennial Analysis of Serious Case Reviews 2005–07.* Available at http://dera.ioe.ac.uk/11151/1/DCSF-RR129(R).pdf, accessed on 10 February 2016.

Brandon, M. (2012) *New Learning from serious case reviews: a two year report for 2009–2011.* Department for Education. Research Report DFE .RR226. London: Department for Education.

Brown, R., and Ward, H. (2013) *Decision Making within a Child's Timeframe. An Overview of Current Research Evidence for Family Justice Professionals Concerning Child Development and the Impact of Maltreatment.* Working Paper 16 (Second edition). London: Thomas Coram Research Unit/Child Wellbeing Research Centre.

Burgess, C., *et al.* (2010) 'It's just like another home, just like another family, so it's nae different. Children's voices in a research study about the experience of children in kinship care in Scotland.' *Child & Family Social Work 15,* 3, 297–306.

C4EO (n.d.) *Safeguarding Expert Briefings.* Available at www.c4eo.org.uk/themes/safeguarding.

Carpenter, B. *et al.* (2014) *Fetal Alcohol Spectrum Disorders, Interdisciplinary Perspectives.* London: Routledge.

Chaudry, M.A., Sherlock, K., and Patel, K. (1997) *Drugs and Ethnic Health Project: Oldham and Tameside.* Preston: University of Central Lancashire.

Children in Scotland (2011) *Fetal Alcohol Harm. The Early Years – What Practitioners and Policy Makers Need to Know.* Briefing Paper 1. Available at www.scottish.parliament.uk/S4_FinanceCommittee/Children_in_Scotland_supp. pdf, accessed on 10 February 2016.

Cleaver, H. *et al.* (1999). *Children's Needs-Parenting Capacity: Child Abuse, Parental Mental Illness, Substance Misuse and Domestic Violence. 1st ed.* London: TSO.

Cleaver, H. *et al.* (2007). *Children's Needs-Parenting Capacity: Child Abuse, Parental Mental Illness, Substance Misuse and Domestic Violence. 2nd ed.* London: TSO.

Cleaver, H., Unell, I., and Aldgate, J. (2011) *Children's Needs – Parenting Capacity: Child Abuse, Parental Mental Illness, Learning Disability, Substance Misuse and Domestic Violence* (Second edition). London: TSO. Available at www.gov.uk/ government/uploads/system/uploads/attachment_data/file/182095/DFE-00108-2011-Childrens_Needs_ Parenting_Capacity.pdf, accessed on 10 February 2016.

Corbett, V. (2005) '"I just knew to keep it quiet…": living with parental problematic substance use.' *Adoption and Fostering 29,* 1, 98–100.

Cosh, J. (2004) 'Talk about it.' *Nursery World 104,* 3946, 28.

Davidson, G., Bunting, L., and Webb, M.A. (2012) *Families Experiencing Multiple Adversities: A Review of the Literature.* Belfast: Barnardo's NI.

Dawe, S., *et al.* (2008) *Improving Outcomes for Children Living in Families with Substance Misuse. What Do We Know and What Should We Do?* Australian Institute of Family Studies. Available at https://aifs.gov.au/cfca/publications/ improving-outcomes-children-living-families-pare, accessed on 9 February 2016.

Dearden, S., and Becker, C. (2000) 'Young Carers in the UK: research, policy and practice.' *Research Planning and Policy 2,* 13–22.

Delargy, A., Shenker, D., Manning, J., and Rickard, A. (2010) *Swept Under the Carpet. Children Affected by Parental Alcohol Misuse.* London: Alcohol Concern.

Department of Health and Others (2000) *Framework for the Assessment of Children in Need and Their Families.* London: Stationery Office.

DSCF, NTA, DH (2009) *Joint Guidance on the Development of Local Protocols between Drug and Alcohol Treatment Services and Local Safeguarding and Family Services.* London: DCSF.

Eiden, R.D. and Leonard, K.E. (2000). 'Parental alcoholism , parental psychopathology and aggravation with infants.' *Journal of Substance Abuse 11,* 1, 17–29.

Falkov, A. (1996) *Fatal Child Abuse and Parental Psychiatric Disorder.* London: Department of Health.

Forrester, D. (2004) 'Social Work Assessments with Parents who Misuse Drugs or Alcohol.' In R. Phillips (ed.) *Children Exposed to Parental Substance Misuse: Implications for Family Placement.* London: BAAF.

Forrester, D. (2012) *Parents Affected by Parental Substance Misuse.* London: BAAF.

Forrester, D., and Harwin, J. (2004) 'Social Work and Parental Substance Misuse.' In R. Phillips (ed.) *Children Exposed to Parental Substance Misuse: Implications for Family Placement.* London: BAAF.

FORUT (2015) *Childhood Matters: Alcohol and Drug Problems from a Child's Rights Perspective.* Available at www.add-resources.org/alcohol-and-drug-problems-from-a-child-rights-perspective.5800210-315773.html, accessed on 10 February 2016.

Fountain, J., *et al.* (2003) *Black and Minority Ethnic Communities in England: A Review of the Literature on Drug Use and Related Service Provision.* London: National Treatment Agency.

FRANK (2005) *Resources Needed to Support Children of Problematic Users of Drugs.* London: COI Communications and Home Office.

Galvani, S. (2015) *Alcohol and Other Drug Use: The Roles and Capabilities of Social Workers.* Manchester: Manchester Metropolitan University.

Galavani, S. and Forrester, D. (2011) 'How well prepared are newly qualified social workers for working with substance us issues. Findings from a National Survey.' *Social Work Education 30,* 4, 422–439.

Galvani, S., and Allnock, D. (2014) 'The nature and extent of substance use education in qualifying social work programmes in England.' *Social Work Education: The International Journal – Special Issue 33,* 5, 573–589.

Glendinning, C., *et al.* (2008) 'Progress and problems in developing outcomes-focused social care services for older people in England.' *Health & Social Care in the Community 16,* 54–63.

Gorin, S. (2004) *Understanding What Children Say about Living with Domestic Violence, Parental Substance Misuse or Parental Health Problems.* York: Joseph Rowntree Foundation.

Gorin, S. (2005) 'The stakes are high: the impact of parental substance misuse on children.' *Childright 219 (September),* 14–16.

Harbin, F. (2006). In F. Harbin and M. Murphy (eds) *Secret Lives: Growing with Substance: Working with Children and Young People Affected by Familial Substance Misuse.* Lyme Regis: Russell House Publishing.

Harocopos, A., *et al.* (2003) *On the Rocks: A Follow-Up Study of Crack Users in London.* London: City Roads, South Bank University, National Treatment Agency.

Harwin, J. (2010) 'Applying the 5-step method to children and families and substance misuse. Opportunities and challenges within policy and practice.' *Drugs Education, Prevention and Policy 17,* 51, 179–192.

Harwin, J., and Forrester, D. (2002) *Parental Substance Misuse and Child Welfare: A Study of Social Work with Families in which Parents Misuse Drugs or Alcohol.* Interim Report. London: Nuffield Foundation.

Hill, L. (2011a) *Children Living with Parental Drug and Alcohol Misuse.* Stirling: Scottish Child Care and Protection Network, University of Stirling.

Hill, L. (2011b) 'Revealing Lives: A Qualitative Study with Children and Young People Affected by Alcohol Problems.' PhD Social Policy. University of Edinburgh.

HM Government (2013, 2015) *Working Together to Safeguard Children.* London: HM Government.

Home Office (2014) *Multi-agency working and information sharing project. Final Report.* London: Home Office.

Homila, M., Itapuisto, M., and Iliva, M. (2011) 'Invisible victims or competent agents: opinion and ways of coping among children aged 12–18 years old with problem drinking parents.' *Drugs: Education, Prevention and Policy 18,* 3, 179–186.

Horgan, J. (2011) *Parental Substance Misuse: Addressing Its Impact on Children. A Review of the Literature.* Dublin: National Advisory Committee on Drugs.

Houmoller, K., *et al.* (2011) *Juggling Harms: Coping with Parental Substance Misuse.* London: London School of Hygiene and Tropical Medicine (Social Care Online).

IRISS (Institute for Research and Innovation in Social Services (n.d.) *Leading for Outcomes: Parental Substance Misuse.* Available at www.iriss.org.uk/resources/leading-outcomes-parental-substance-misuse, accessed on 10 February 2016.

ISPCC (2011) *ISPCC highlights alcohol abuse as a child protection issue.* Available at www.ispcc.ie, accessed on 10 February 2016.

Johnson, M.R.D., and Carroll, M. (1995) *Dealing with Diversity: Good Practice in Drug Prevention Work with Racially and Culturally Diverse Communities.* London: Home Office.

Kahler, C.W. et al. (2003) 'Sources of distress among women in treatment with their alcoholic partners.' *Journal of Substance Abuse Treatment 24,* 257–265.

Kearney, J., Harbin, F., Murphy, M., Wheeler, E., and Whittle, J. (2005) *The Highs and Lows of Family Life: Familial Substance Misuse from a Child's Perspective.* Bolton: Bolton Substance Misuse Research Group.

Kroll, B. (2004) 'Living with an elephant: growing up with parental substance misuse.' *Child and Family Social Work 9,* 129–140.

Kroll, B. (2007) 'A family affair? Kinship care and parental substance misuse.' *Child and Family Social Work 12,* 1, 84–93.

Kroll, B., and Taylor, A. (2003) *Parental Substance Misuse and Child Welfare.* London: Jessica Kingsley Publishers.

Kroll, B. and Taylor, A. (2004) 'Working With Parental Substance Misuse: Dilemmas for Practice.' *British Journal of Social Work, 34,* 8.

Kroll, B., and Taylor, A. (2008) *The Impact of Parental Substance Misuse in Child Development.* Research in Practice/ Frontline. www.rip.org.uk.

Laslett, A.-M., Room, R., Dietze, P., and Ferris, J. (2012) 'Alcohol's involvement in concurrent child abuse and neglect cases.' *Addiction 107,* 10, 1786–1793.

Lea, A. (2011) *Families with Complex Needs: A Review of Current Literature.* Leicester: Leicestershire County Council

Lloyds TSB Foundation for Scotland and the Scottish Government (n.d.) *Drugs Initiative – Recovery and Children Project.* Available at www.ltsbfoundationforscotland.org.uk, accessed on 10 February 2016.

Manning, J., Clifton, J., and McDonald, C. (2014) *'I Think You Need Someone to Show You What Help There Is.' Parental Alcohol Misuse – Uncovering and Responding to Children's Needs at a Local Level.* London: Office of the Children's Commissioner.

Manning, V., *et al.* (2009) 'New estimates of the number of children living with substance misusing parents: results from national household surveys.' *BMC Public Health 9,* 377–388.

McAleavy, S., Pearson, H., and Sloan, H. (2004) *Can You See the Elephant? A Toolkit for Talking to Children and Young People About Parental Substance Use.* Leicester: Leicestershire Partnership NHS Trust, Leicester City Council and DRUG Alcohol Response Team.

Moe, J., *et al.* (2008) 'Evaluation of the Betty Ford Children's Program.' *Journal of Social Work Practice in the Addictions 8,* 4, 464–489.

Munro, E. (2011) *The Munro Review of Child Protection. Final Report. A Child Centred System.* London: TSO.

Murphy, M., and Harbin, F. (2003) 'The Assessment of Parental Substance Misuse and Its Impact on Childcare.' In M. Calder and S. Hackett (eds) *Assessment in Child Care: Using and Developing Frameworks for Practice.* Lyme Regis: Russell House Publishing.

National Risk Framework to Support the Assessment of Children and Young People (n.d.). Calder M et al in partnership with Garth Associates. NHS Choices –Your Health, Your Choices www.nhs.uk/pages/home.aspx

NTA (2005) *Working with Drug Using Parents: Training Manual.* Competency Based Training Module SD19. Available at www.nta.nhs.uk.

NTA (2012) *Medications in Recovery – Re-Orientating Drug Dependence Treatment.* Available at www.nta.nhs.uk/uploads/medications-in-recovery-main-report3.pdf, accessed on 10 February 2016.

Office for National Statistics (2016) *Alcohol-Related Deaths in the UK, 2014.* Available at www.ons.gov.uk/ons/rel/subnational-health4/alcohol-related-deaths-in-the-united-kingdom/2014/index.html, accessed on 10 February 2016.

Ofsted (2010) *Learning lessons from serious case reviews 2009–2010.* Manchester: Ofsted.

Ofsted (2011) *Ages of Concern: Learning Lessons from Serious Case Reviews.* London: Ofsted.

Petch, A. et al. (2012) *Audit and Analysis of Significant Case Reviews.* Edinburgh: Scottish Government.

Phillips, R. (ed.) (2004) *Children Exposed to Parental Substance Misuse: Implications for Family Placement.* London: BAAF.

Public Health England (2010). Drug and Alcohol News 2010.

Public Health England (2015) *Local Initiatives in Safeguarding, Sheffield and Lewisham: Safeguarding and Substance Misuse.*

Radcliffe, P. (2011) 'Motherhood, pregnancy and the negotiation of identity: the moral career of drug treatment.' *Social Science and Medicine 72,* 6, 984–991.

Ramsey, M., *et al.* (2001) *Drug Misuse Declared in 2000: Results from the British Crime Survey.* London: Home Office Research, Development and Statistics Directorate.

RCM (2010) *Alcohol and Pregnancy Guidance Paper.* London: The Royal College of Midwives.

Reder, P., and Duncan, S. (1999) *Lost Innocents: A Follow-Up Study of Fatal Child Abuse.* London: Routledge.

Riley, E. (2011) *The Fetal Brain and Alcohol: Defining Fetal Alcohol Syndrome Disorder (FASD).* Paper Presentation at 'Bruised before Birth' TACT Conference, Edinburgh.

SAMHSA/CSAT (2009). *Addressing the special needs of women. Treatment Improvement Protocol (TIP).* Series No. 51 Rockville (MD).

Sangster, D., *et al.* (2002) *Delivering Drug Services to Black and Minority Ethnic Communities.* London: Drug Prevention Advisory Service.

Scottish Executive/Government (2003, 2013) *Getting Our Priorities Right: Good Practice Guidance for Working with Children and Families Affected by Substance Misuse.* Edinburgh: Scottish Executive/Government.

Scottish Executive (2006) *Hidden Harm: Next Steps: Supporting Children – Working with Parents.* Edinburgh: Scottish Executive.

Scottish Government (2009) *The Early Years Framework.* Edinburgh: Scottish Government.

Scottish Government (2015) *The Early Years Collaborative.* Edinburgh: Scottish Government.

Seval Brooks, C. and Rice, K.F. (1997) *Families in Recovery: Coming Full Circle.* Baltimore: Brookes Publishing Co.

Selwyn, J., Farmer, E., Meakings, S., and Vaisey, P. (2015) *The Poor Relations? Children and Informal Kinship Carers Speak Out.* Bristol: University of Bristol.

Sloper, P. (2004) 'Facilitators and barriers for coordinated multi-agency services.' *Child Care, Health and Development 30,* 6, 571–580.

Social Care Institute for Excellence (2004) *Research Briefing 06: Parenting Capacity and Substance Misuse.* London: SCIE.

Statham, J. (2004) 'Effective services to support children in special circumstances.' *Child Care, Health and Development 30*, 6, 589–598.

Tallon, V., and Barlow, J. (2012) *Developing a Blueprint for an Alcohol and Drug Workforce Development Model in North Lanarkshire.* Lanarkshire: Alcohol and Drug Partnership.

Taylor, A., and Kroll, B. (2004) 'Working with parental substance misuse: dilemmas for practice.' *British Journal of Social Work 34*, 1115–1132.

Taylor, J., and Lazenbatt, A. (2014) *Child Maltreatment and High Risk Families: Protecting Children and Young People.* Edinburgh: Dunedin Press.

Templeton, L. (2012) *Supporting Young People Affected by Parental Substance Misuse and/or Parental Mental Health. Problems in Northern Ireland: Evaluation of the Pilot Study.* ASCERT, HSC Southern Eastern Health and Social Care Trust, Barnardo's, HSC Public Health Agency.

Templeton, L. (2013) *Embracing Children and Families in Substance Misuse Treatment.* In W. Mistral (ed.) *Emerging Perspectives on Substance Misuse.* Oxford: Wiley-Blackwell.

Turning Point (2006) *Bottling It Up: The Effects of Alcohol Misuse on Children, Parents and Families.* London: Turning Point.

Turning Point (2011) *Bottling It Up: The Next Generation.* Available at www.turning-point.co.uk/media/53899/bottlingitup.2011.pdf, accessed on 27 June 2016

UK Drugs Policy Commission (2008) *A Vision of Recovery: UKDPC Recovery Consensus Group.* London: UKDPC.

Velleman, R. and Orford, J. (1999). *Risk and Resilience: Adults who were the children of problem drinkers.* Amsterdam: Harwood Academic.

Velleman, R., and Templeton, L. (2007) 'Understanding and modifying the impact of parents' substance misuse on children.' *Advances in Psychiatric Treatment 13*, 2, 79–89.

Vincent, S., and Petch, A. (2012) *Audit and Analysis of Significant Case Reviews.* Glasgow: IRISS.

Wales, A., *et al.* (2009). *Untold Damage: Children's Accounts of Living with Harmful Parental Drinking.* Edinburgh: Scottish Health Action for Alcohol Problems and ChildLine Scotland.

White, W. (2011) Celebrating the Varieties of Recovery Experience. White House Office of Drug Control Policy, available at www.whitehouse.gov/ondcp/blog